⊄ **W9-AXH-536**

③

DREAMCATCHERS

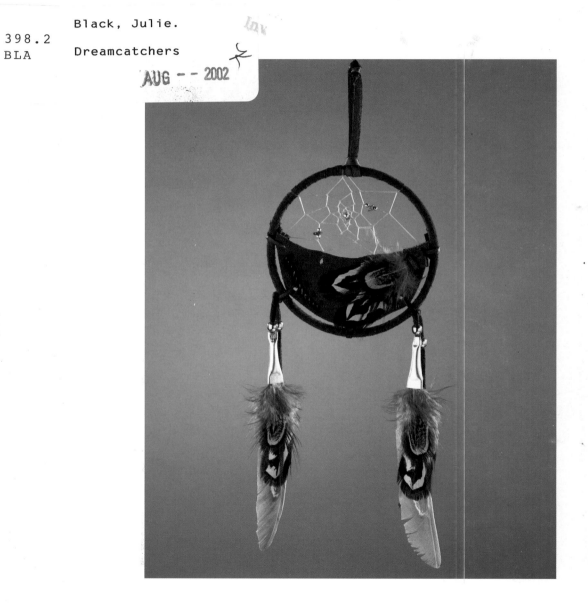

DREAM CATCHERS

Myths and History

JULIE BLACK

FIREFLY BOOKS

A FIREFLY BOOK

Published by Firefly Books Ltd. 1999

Library of Congress Cataloguing in Publication Data

Dreamcatchers: myths and history / Julie Black.—1st ed.

[128]p.: col. ill.; cm.
Summary: The history of Ojibway dreamcatchers, plus how to make one.
ISBN 1-55209-439-1
1. Ojibway Indians – Legends. 2. Dreams – Folklore. I. Title.
398.2/ 098/ 973–dc21   1999   CIP

First Printing

Published in the United States in 1999 by
Firefly Books (U.S.) Inc.
P.O. Box 1338, Ellicott Station
Buffalo, New York, USA
14205

Electronic formatting: Jean Lightfoot Peters

Researched by: Julie V. Gottlieb

Printed and bound in Italy

Photo Credits: All photographs from Talewinds Arts & Crafts and Whetungs Art Gallery, and those appearing on pages 15 and 20 © Michael Cullen, Trent Photographics. The dreamcatchers appearing on the following pages were kindly supplied by Tanya Maracle and Linda Parker of Talewinds Arts & Crafts: 1, 2, 5, 6, 34, 13, 14, 49, 51, 52, 56, 65, 72, 81, 84, 91, 103, 106, 122, 124. All items appearing on the following pages were kindly supplied by Michael Whetung of Whetungs Art Gallery, Peterborough, Ontario, Canada: 46, 55, 59, 62, 67, 74, 79, 96, 108, 110, 114, 113. Page 9: National Archives of Canada / PA-181609. Page 11: Glenbow Archives / NA-1570-2. Page 17: Pemrose & Bowles / Glenbow Archives / NA-4406-2. Page 23: T.C. Weston / National Archives of Canada / PA-050793. Page 26: Glenbow Archives / NA-1406-99. Page 44: National Archives of Canada / PA-181544. Page 76: Glenbow Archives / NA-1681-6. Page 86: Glenbow Archives / NA-1406-170. Page 59: Dreamcatcher by Brad Kavanaugh, courtesy of Whetung's Arts & Crafts. Page 125-6: "How to Make a Dreamcatcher" Illustrations from page 125-6 © Nazy Sakhavarz.

Page 31:
Norval Morrisseau 1931-
Shaman and Disciples 1979
acrylic on canvas
180.5 x 211.5 cm
McMichael Canadian Art Collection
Purchase 1979
1979.34.7

Contents

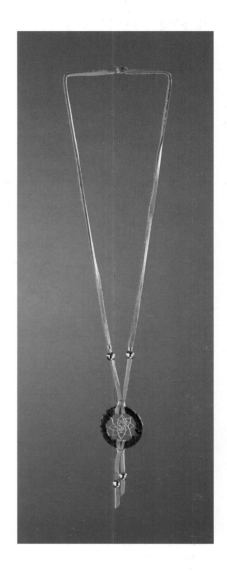

The Ojibway People

EW SYMBOLS CAPTURE SO WELL THE VALUES AND complex belief system of the Ojibway people as does the dreamcatcher. Born of legend, this beautiful hooped-web talisman has for centuries shielded Ojibway children from bad dreams and negative influences.

For the Ojibway, dreams play an integral role in all aspects and through all phases of life. The messages that can be accessed only through dreaming are regarded as among the more important lessons we learn during our time here on earth. In fact, the Ojibway word for dream—*bawedjigewin*—also means vision. So the dreamcatcher holds a special place in Ojibway life. The infant's dreamcatcher is his or her very first protective device; it both protects the child and unites him or her to tribal values. Later, a young boy's first step towards adulthood will be marked by the rite of passage known as the Dream Quest.

The dreamcatcher is not a historical relic. Just as Ojibway culture continues to flourish and has seen many rebirths, so the dreamcatcher remains a living and continually evolving part of Ojibway culture. Today, dreamcatchers can be seen anywhere Native art is exhibited—art galleries, craft shows, even on the Internet! First Nations artisans craft ever-new versions of dreamcatchers.

One of the largest First Nations tribes north of the Mexican border, the Ojibway have continued to flourish and their culture has seen many rebirths. Today, many Ojibway are embracing their old traditions and customs in order to reconnect with their cultural legacy.

Dreamcatchers still serve their original purpose of protecting the young from bad dreams, and in schools, in art classes and at home, they are now being made by children of many cultures. In an age of disturbing visions, the dreamcatcher has begun to attract an ever-widening public. It is not at all unusual these days to see dreamcatchers hung in windows, over beds and even on car windshields.

With so many applications in our own world, it is fascinating to trace the cultural origins and the history from which the dreamcatcher has emerged to capture our imagination.

History of the First or Original Man

The Ojibway, or Ojibwe, were one of the largest First Nations tribes north of the Mexican border. Together with the Montagnais, Naskapi, Abenaki, Ottawa, Algonquin and Cree, the Ojibway language belongs to the Algonquian family of languages. It was only upon the arrival of the white man in their ancestral territory that these people began to refer to themselves, when in the presence of the white man, as the "Ojibway." The word "Ojibway" is commonly translated as "puckering." One theory about this reference to puckering relates it to the style of moccasins worn by the Ojibway. The seams of Ojibway moccasins were sewn in such a way as to "pucker," and it is thought that the

Ojibway were thus given this name by neighboring tribes. Most historical records, particularly those recounting the stories of Ojibway
elders, acknowledge the moccasin translation as the true origin of the
word "Ojibway." When the first European explorers met the Ojibway,
they misunderstood the pronunciation of their tribal name, labeling
them "Chippewa," and it was by this name that they were called well

The Ojibway were originally a nomadic people. Today they still comprise a number of widespread bands and self-governing tribes. Each tribe was subdivided into bands, which were politically independent from one another.

into the 20th century. Like so much that was lost in translation and through forced acculturation after the European invasion, it is only now that the Ojibway have reappropriated their native name, "Anishinaubae." Anishinaubae is derived from the following root forms: *ani*, meaning whence; *nishina*, meaning lowered; and *abe*, meaning the male of the species. Anishinaubae has been translated as "First Male," "First Man" or "Original Man." According to the Ojibway Creation story, the Original Man was lowered to the Earth and all North American tribes came from him.

The ancestors of the Ojibway made up part of the original human settlement of the North American continent. The Ojibway believe that their people were born in North America while the continent itself was still in its infancy. This conviction differs from that of conservative scholars who maintain that the North American Indians' place of origin is somewhere in Asia and that the Indians came to North America via the Bering Strait anywhere from 10,000 to 25,000 years ago. This theory is at odds with more recent scholarly studies and discoveries suggesting that humans have inhabited this continent far longer than was first believed, possibly as long as 250,000 years.

There are many different versions of the legend about the origin of the Ojibway/Anishinaubae people in North America. This is one of the many popular legends. Long ago, the Kitchi-Manitou (the

Great Mystery or Great Creator) first peopled the Earth. The Anishinaubae, or Original People, however, strayed from their harmonious ways and began to argue and fight with one another. Brother turned against brother, and soon the Anishinaubae were killing one another over hunting grounds and other disagreements. Seeing that harmony, brotherhood, sisterhood and respect for all living things no longer prevailed on Earth, Kitchi-Manitou decided to purify the Earth. He did this with Water.

The water came in the form of a great flood, or mush-ko'-be-wun', upon the Earth which destroyed the Anishinaubae people and most of the animals as well. Only Nana'b'oozoo, the central figure in many of the Anishinaubae oral traditions, was able to survive the flood, along with a few animals and birds who managed to swim in the water or fly above it. Nana'b'oozoo floated on a huge log searching for land, but none was to be found as the Earth was now covered by the great flood. Nana'b'oozoo allowed the remaining animals and birds to take turns resting on the log. Finally, Nana'b'oozoo spoke:

"I am going to do something," he said. "I am going to swim to the bottom of this water and grab a handful of Earth. With this small bit of Earth, I believe we can create a new land for us to live on with the help of the Four Winds and Kitchi-Manitou."

So Nana'b'oozoo dove into the water and was gone for a long time. Finally he surfaced, and, short of breath, he told the animals that the water was too deep for him to swim to the bottom. All were silent. Finally, Mahng, the Loon, spoke up. "I can dive under the water for a long way. That is how I catch my food. I will try to make it to the bottom and return with some Earth in my beak."

The Loon disappeared and was gone for a very long time. Surely, thought the others, the Loon must have drowned. Then they saw him float to the surface, weak and nearly unconscious. "I couldn't make it. There must be no bottom to this water," he gasped.

Then Zhing-gi-biss, the helldiver, came forward and said, "I

will try next. Everyone knows I can dive great distances." So the helldiver went under. Again, a very long time passed, and the others
thought he was surely drowned. At last he floated to the surface. He
was unconscious, and not until he came to could he relate to the others that he too was unable to fetch the Earth from the bottom of the
water.

Many more animals tried, including Zhon-gwayzh', the mink,
and even Mi-zhee-kay', the turtle. All failed, and it seemed as though
there would never be a way to get the much-needed Earth from the
bottom of the water. Then a soft, muffled voice was heard. "I can do
it," it said softly. At first no one could see who it was that spoke up.
Then the little Wa-zhushk', the muskrat, stepped forward. "I will try,"
he repeated. Some of the bigger, more powerful animals laughed at the
little muskrat. Nana'b'oozoo spoke up. "Only Kitchi-Manitou can
place judgment on others. If muskrat wants to try, he should be
allowed to."

So, muskrat dove into the water. He was gone much longer than
any of the others. After a while Nana'b'oozoo and the other animals
were certain that muskrat had given his life trying to reach the bottom.
Far below the water's surface, however, muskrat had, in fact, reached
the bottom. Very weak from lack of air, he grabbed some Earth in his
paw and, with all the energy he could muster, began to swim upward.

Perhaps no other symbol so readily identifies the Ojibway culture as the birchbark canoe. A very old tradition that is again being embraced by contemporary Ojibway, the craft of making birchbark canoes was at one time taught to all young Ojibway as a matter of course.

One of the animals spotted muskrat as he floated to the surface. Nana'b'oozoo pulled him up onto the log.

"Brothers and sisters," Nana'b'oozoo said, "muskrat went too long without air. He is dead." A song of mourning and praise was heard across the water as muskrat's spirit passed on to the spirit world. Suddenly Nana'b'oozoo exclaimed, "Look, there is something in his paw!" Nana'b'oozoo carefully opened the tiny paw. All the animals gathered close to see what was held so tightly there. Muskrat's paw opened and revealed a small ball of Earth. The animals all shouted with joy. Muskrat had sacrificed his life so that life on Earth could begin anew.

Nana'b'oozoo took the piece of Earth from Muskrat's paw. Just then, the turtle swam forward and said, "Use my back to bear the weight of this piece of Earth. With the help of Kitchi-Manitou, we can make a new Earth." Nana'b'oozoo put the piece of Earth on the turtle's back. Suddenly, the wind blew from each of the Four Directions, North, South, East and West. The tiny piece of Earth on turtle's back began to grow. It grew and grew and grew until it formed a mi-ni-si', or island, in the water. The island grew larger and larger, but still the turtle bore the weight of the Earth on his back. Nana'b'oozoo and the animals all sang and danced in a widening circle on the growing island. After a while, the Four Winds ceased to blow

and the waters became still. A huge island sat in the middle of the water, and today that island is known as North America, the Land of the Great Turtle or Turtle Island, because it is shaped like a turtle (Florida is one hind leg, Baja California is another, Mexico is the tail).

Traditional Indian people, including the Ojibway, hold special reverence for the muskrat who sacrificed his life and made life possible for the Earth's second people. To this day, the muskrat has been given a good life. No matter that marshes have been drained and the muskrat's homes destroyed in the name of progress; the muskrat continues to survive and multiply. The muskrats do their part today in remembering the great flood: they build their homes in the shape of the little ball of Earth and the island that was formed from it.

A nomadic people comprising a number of widespread bands and self-governing tribes, the Ojibway survived and prospered by fishing, hunting and, later, cultivating corn (thought to have been taught them by the Huron). The Ojibway were skilled hunters and trappers. With bows and arrows and snares, they hunted moose, beaver, bear, rabbit, marten, deer and wild birds. The meat provided sustenance, and the skins, bones and feathers were each used to construct shelters and make tools and indoor furnishings. In addition to this, the Ojibway people were homemakers, healers, storytellers and (but only as a last resort) warriors. Their major purpose in life was to survive as

individuals and communities, and it was survival that preoccupied their lives.

In the spring they would clear a patch of land to plant corn seeds. The Ojibway diet was the most varied during the summer: women collected berries and fruit, and all harvested wild rice from the marshes; this was also the best hunting season. In the autumn they returned to the corn patch for the harvest. In winter they cut holes in the ice and, using lures of carved wooden minnows, speared the fish when they took the bait. In late winter the Ojibway tapped the maple trees for their sap, and boiled it down to maple sugar—enjoying sweets during the seasons when fresh fruit was not available.

The Ojibway faced formidable odds and impediments in their lives. Nevertheless, despite the rugged lands, vast distances, blizzards and winds, mosquitoes and black flies, personal weaknesses and failings, the Ojibway people roamed the land and plied the lakes and rivers in quest of food and medicine to nourish themselves. For transportation through the waterways they built birchbark canoes, and their dwelling place was the wigwam, made from deer hides or birchbark and strong branches. All their household and spiritual articles—bows and arrows of limited range, clubs, spears, nets, stone knives and digging sticks—were crafted with portability in mind.

Though the Ojibway were preoccupied with their numerous

material needs and wants, their mode of life—that is, their simple way of meeting simple needs—was very rewarding and filled them with pride. Without exception, every man and woman had to master the practical skills of curing meat and vegetables, setting nets and traps, making tools and canoes, tanning hides and making clothing, as well as understanding animals and knowing the properties of plants and their parts.

Social Organization

The closely associated Algonquian tribes of the Ojibway, Odawa (Ottawa), Mississauga and Potowatomi share common geographic origins, cultural similarities and related histories. The contemporary remnants of these groups are often considered under the general term "Ojibway." Each tribe was subdivided into bands, which were autonomous and politically independent from one another. Most bands were small groups, the largest numbering only 300 to 400 people. Social organization was determined by a further division according to totems or clans. The totems reflected the needs of Ojibway society: the chiefs provided the community with leadership; the warriors were the bands' defense; the hunters provided nourishment; the

Children were born into their father's totem group. The totem, represented by the totem pole, was more important than family ties, and transcended band and tribal affiliations and loyalties.

teachers were the great storytellers and conservers of tradition; and the medicine men protected the individual and the community against spiritual and physical ailments.

According to Ojibway legend, the Clan System came to be after the great flood and the emergence of the Earth's second people. Kitchi-Manitou remembered the arguments and fights that took place among the Earth's first people. To prevent such disturbances from recurring, Kitchi-Manitou gave the Ojibway a form of government called o-do-i-daym-i-wan', or the Clan System. Into the Clan System was built equal justice and voice, law and order. By its very nature it reinforced the teachings and principles of a sacred way of life. There were seven original Clans: Crane, Loon, Fish, Bear, Martin, Deer and Bird. Many generations later the seven original Clans branched out and sub-Clans were created.

Each Clan was given a special role in the structure and governance of the Ojibway. The Cranes and Loons were given the power of chieftainship, and included the people with natural qualities of leadership. By working together, the two Clans provided the people with balanced leadership, each serving as a check on the other. Between the Crane and Loon Clans stood the Fish Clan, sometimes called the Water Clan. The Fish Clan was made up of the intellectuals of the people. They were sometimes called "star gazers" since they were

An Ojibway camp at Jackfish River near Lake Winnipeg, circa 1884. The Ojibway lived in wigwams made of animal hide and traveled by birchbark canoe. The Ojibway often acted as guides for the European newcomers to North America.

known for their constant pursuit of meditation and philosophy. The Fish Clan members would settle disputes between the two chief Clans. The Bear Clan served as the police force for the people. They spent most of their time patrolling the outskirts of the village so as to be prepared for unwanted visitors. Because of the amount of time they spent in the woods, they became knowledgeable about the various herbs and medicinal plants used in healing. The Martin Clan served as the warriors, protecting at all cost. The Deer Clan were known as the Clan of gentle people. They were the pacifists and poets. The Bird Clan represented the spiritual leaders of the people. They were said to have the characteristics of the eagle, the head of their Clan, because they pursued the higher elevations of the mind just like the eagle pursued the higher elevations of the sky.

According to anthropologists, Ojibway social organization was patrilineal, and children were born into their father's totem group. This lineage system is an anthropological preoccupation, however, and does not serve any real purpose in Ojibway social organization. There has been some speculation that Ojibway bands were matriarchal long ago, and that women held the greater authority in the community. While it has been documented that some Ojibway clans were matrilineal, we now believe that this was the exception rather than the rule. Although children were initially trained in the arts of their totem, there was room to grow if the child displayed extraordinary skill in

another area. Thus the son of a hunter could be accepted into a warrior Clan, or a warrior into a teacher Clan, and so on. Totems were more important than family ties, and transcended band and tribal affiliations and loyalties. Therefore, members of the same totem were as likely to regard each other as sisters and brothers as they were to hold special affection for their blood siblings. In the same way, marriage between a man and woman of the same totem was prohibited.

First Contact

The Ojibway's first contact with French explorers occurred in the early 1600s, and in 1608 the famous French explorer Samuel de Champlain encountered members of the Ojibway and Huron tribes on his westward route along the St. Lawrence. These first encounters were generally friendly. Serving as guides, the Ojibway accompanied Europeans on their expeditions in search of a passage to the Orient, and from an early date they were enthusiastic traders, exchanging mainly much sought-after beaver pelts for the European goods that they valued most, such as firearms and beads.

After 1649, when the Iroquois and Huron nations were scattered, it is widely believed the Ojibway moved into the territory now known as southern Ontario. Continued Ojibway expansion during the period of the first European settlements was dramatic. Some Ojibway bands migrated south into Wisconsin and Minnesota by displacing, sometimes by force, the Dakota tribes. With the lucrative fur trade as their main incentive, other Ojibway bands went far and wide from their Great Lakes base, and spread into the Shield country of northern Ontario and Manitoba in search of new trapping grounds. Still others ventured out onto the Plains, becoming the Plains Ojibway of southern Manitoba and Saskatchewan.

Because they occupied those territories that were most coveted by European explorers and settlers, the history of the Ojibway after 1600 was closely intertwined with that of colonial North America. While this relationship began as mutually beneficial and co-operative, it soon deteriorated and became fraught with violence. In southern Ontario, the Ojibway enjoyed something of a golden age from the beginning to the middle of the 18th century. With virtual control over the Great Lakes area, the Ojibway, as the principal middlemen in the fur trade among aboriginal tribes, could decide whether they should trade with the French, their commercial partners and military allies of long standing, or the newer competition, the English; the choice was made on the basis of who offered the best price. At the same time, the Ojibway were approached by both the French and the English seeking a military alliance. It was only during the 1760s that the Franco-Ojibway alliance broke down, after the French forces were defeated by British forces on the Plains of Abraham (1759).

The 19th century witnessed the increasing domination and marginalization of the aboriginal peoples by European colonialists. The Ojibway of Upper Canada were now outnumbered by the European immigrants, and after the War of 1812 the rapid American settlement of the frontier swept away the Ojibway's traditional allies. Consequently, by the 1820s, it was evident to the Ojibway themselves

Traditional Ojibway communities kept their children close to the parents, both physically and emotionally. Ojibway women would carry their infants on their backs in a tikinagan, pictured here, while they moved and worked around the camp.

that they were running out of land to retreat to, land that remained unspoiled by settlement, that was not subjected to vast deforestation and other interference with the environment, and upon which they could continue to hunt and trap unmolested by land-grabbing colonizers. Therefore, by the end of the decade, most land surrender agreements between the Ojibway and the British government included provisions for Native "reserves."

From its inception, the reserve system and the policy of forced assimilation was endorsed by Euro-Canadian social reformers and missionaries. They wished to see Native people abandon the life of the hunter-gatherer society and become self-supporting farmers. In the 1830s, the most notorious of these early schemes to place the reserves in isolated areas was advocated by Lieutenant-Governor Sir Francis Bond Head, and the first tribe he sought to relocate were the Saugeen River Ojibway. In exchange for 1.5 million acres of their land on the Bruce Peninsula, Bond Head intended to relocate the Ojibway population to Manitoulin Island in Lake Huron. The Saugeen objected and, with the support of church groups and the recently formed, Aborigines' Protection Society (based in London),they were not forced to relocate to the Island. However, the land grab itself was upheld and the Saugeen were forced to accept small reserves on the Bruce Peninsula.

By mid-century, the Ontario Ojibway had signed away most of the fertile region of present-day southern Ontario, and by the 1850s they were left with only a few barren offshore islands in the Bruce Peninsula that they could call home. Even when the Ojibway had made the successful shift to becoming farmers, there was little protection against the hearty appetite of the new pioneers for land. The fate of the Credit River Mississaugas, who had started to make a success of farming their land but who were nevertheless under threat of relocation, is a case in point. Joseph Sawyer (Kawahjegezhegwabe), chief of the Credit River band, described the impossible situation in which his people found themselves:

> Now we raise our own corn, potatoes, wheat; we have cattle, and many comforts, and conveniences. But if we go to Maneetoolin, we could not live; soon we should be extinct as a people; we could raise no potatoes, corn, pork, or beef; nothing would grow by putting the seed on the smooth rock.[1]

While the Credit River band were not relocated to the isolated island, they were nonetheless compelled to abandon their title to their land and accept an offer to move to the Grand River Valley.

The Indian Act

In 1860 the British relinquished control of Indian Affairs to the Canadian government, and in 1876 Parliament introduced the Indian Act. The Indian Act made a more assertive effort at forced assimilation of the Native peoples into Euro-Canadian society. In this period the church-controlled Native school system was expanded. Even when the school was situated on the reserve, students were punished for speaking their Ojibway language. Most disastrous of all were the residential schools, also run by Christian missionaries, which required children to leave their tight-knit community and families. In traditional Ojibway communities, parents tended to keep their children very close both physically and emotionally. We can imagine, then, how traumatic it was for parent and child to be torn asunder when the young were compelled to attend church-run boarding schools where the student was subjected to brutal discipline and sexual violence, fed a poor diet and prohibited from retaining the history and beliefs of the Ojibway.

While the Grand Council of the Ojibway of southern Ontario gathered bi-annually in an attempt to consolidate a united front against government authoritarianism, their influence was minimal. Progressively during the 19th century, the economic development of the reserves was thwarted; only if the Ojibway turned to farming were

Shaman and Disciples, 1979, by Norval Morrisseau. His paintings often depict the spirituality of the Ojibway people, and are particularly known for their use of bright and vivid colors.

they encouraged by the government. Fishing and forestry, even on their own land, was taken out of Native hands and contracted to Euro-Canadians.

The two world wars of the 20th century marked a turning point in Ojibway resolve and fighting spirit. It is claimed that in the First and Second World Wars "no other ethnic group in Canada contributed a greater proportion of their men to the defeat of the enemy,"[2] and yet only in 1960 were members of Canada's First Nations enfranchised. With the force of long-delayed citizenship have come strong demands for self-government, self-determination and the end to an often cruel policy of forced assimilation and acculturation.

It has been estimated that in the period before European contact all the Ojibway bands together numbered fewer than 3000 individuals. During the 1940s it was estimated that some 30,000 Ojibway lived in the United States and some 15,000 in Canada. In 1998, Canadian government statistics show that approximately 20,000 Ojibway live on three dozen reserves scattered throughout southern Ontario. The Ojibway are considered the most numerous group of First Nations people in the province.

In our own time, many talented and creative Canadian Natives have gained national and international recognition in the arts. While discrimination and racism are still the regrettable realities that Native people often face when they move to cities and other multi-ethnic

Canadian communities, there is an increasing appreciation for their gifts, their history and their unique vision. Among those Ojibway who have risen to prominence are the renowned painter Norval Morriseau and the writer Basil Johnston. Not only have they introduced the spirit, spirituality, oral tradition and lush esthetic of their people to a wider public, but also, by so doing, they have asserted the wonder and beauty of this ancient culture to the rest of the world. In 1993 the National Aboriginal Awards were established to honor excellence and achievement among First Nations people.

Today, instead of being shrouded in protective secrecy and shame, many First Nations people are embracing their past. For instance, the Iroquois Nation of the Woodland Cultural Centre in Brantford, Ontario, has transformed a former residential school into a museum to educate all visitors. First Nations people across Canada are demanding government recognition, the righting of past wrongs and compensation for persecution, exclusion and eviction from their own land.

Life of the Spirit

Throughout their long history, and despite the devastating aftermath of European contact, the Ojibway continued with a spiritual life that

is based on an earlier animistic world view. The majority of anthropologists agree that the supernatural world dominated the way in which
the Ojibway viewed reality. Seeing themselves as existing in a closely
knit community of human persons, animal persons and other-than-
human persons, spiritual expression was governed by the need to
respect each of these members and to offend no one. The fundamental
essence of Ojibway life is unity—the oneness of all things. According
to the Ojibway, history is expressed in the way that life is lived each
day. Key to this is the belief that harmony with all created things has
been achieved. The people cannot be separated from the land, with its
cycle of seasons, or from the other mysterious cycles of living
things—birth and growth and death and new birth; where they come
from is integral to Ojibway life. Their story is deep within their hearts.
It is the story of the spirit, both the individual and the collective.

Scholars and anthropologists differ on the origins of Ojibway
spirituality, with many believing that material needs were paramount
to Ojibway life. On the contrary, however, according to many Natives,
such as Basil Johnston, it is precisely because of the Ojibway's simple
existence through the centuries that an abundant spiritual life was
awakened and developed in Ojibway man and woman. The Ojibway's
close relationship with nature developed a consciousness that there
were realities and presences in life other than the corporeal and the

A modern Ojibway dreamcatcher. The Ojibway believed very strongly in the oneness of all things. An integral part of this belief was that harmony exists between all created things.

material. The spirit, "Manitou," which can be roughly translated as "the mystery," is a part of life and cannot not be separated from it. The Manitou refers to realities other than the physical ones of rock, fire, water, air, wood and flesh—it refers to the unseen realities of individual beings, places and events that are beyond human understanding but are still clearly real. It is to the Manitous that Ojibway men and women turn in their vision quests and purification rites for the betterment of their inner beings.

In general terms, Ojibway spirituality centers around certain customs and beliefs, concepts, events and objects. These include the sweatlodge, pipe, drums, singing, the naming ceremony, prayer, vision questing and guardian spirits, the Pow Wow, the medicine man or woman (shamans), medicine bags, dream articles and traditional stories regarding the Great Spirit, Creation, Original Man and The Flood, among many others. Ritual and spiritual objects include things like sage, sweetgrass, tobacco and cedar, and these objects were often used in various Ojibway ceremonies in order to make contact with the spiritual world.

The number four is sacred to Ojibway spirituality and figures prominently in the culture, religion, prophecies and oral traditions (stories) for most North American Indian tribes. The number four refers to what is known as the Four Colors. Although there may be some variations from tribe to tribe, basically the Four Colors represent the Four cardinal or sacred Directions: North, East, South and West. The Four Colors also represent the Four Colors of the human race: White, Yellow, Red and Black and the Four Elements: Earth, Water, Fire and Air. In addition to the Four Colors, the color Green is often used to represent Mother Earth, and the color Blue is used in place of Black to represent Water.

Each of the Four Directions hold a special meaning to the Ojibway. Briefly, North represents strength, stamina and endurance; East marks the beginning of the life cycle, for it is where the Sun first rises, and it also symbolizes wisdom and knowledge; South represents change, as the southern winds bring forth a seasonal renewal to the Earth; in the West lies the path of souls, where the Indian must cross a large body of water or a river in order for his or her soul to enter the spirit world, leaving the human form behind to become one with the Earth, thus repeating the cycle of life and death and renewal. Many variations and interpretations of the Four Directions can be found among the more than 300 American Indian and Canadian First Nation tribes across Turtle Island, or North America, but all are integral to the understanding of the spiritual life of the Ojibway.

Ojibway tradition indicates that the Great Spirit "told them how to act; and with this knowledge they think it would be wrong, and give great offence to their Creator, to forsake the old ways of their forefathers."[3] The precarious nature of life through hunting, and eventually through warfare as well, also put a great deal of emphasis on the Ojibway's ability to control the supernatural. The hunter-warrior's speed, accuracy, concealment, endurance and strength, for example, were attributed to the individual's understanding of the Manitous and his ability to please them. This relationship was in most cases practical, since myriad Manitou spirits were to be found in the sky, hills, animals, birds, trees, lakes, rivers and streams, and it allowed the successful hunter or warrior to brag among his peers without seeming egotistical, since he was, in effect, praising his gods. No important expedition against an enemy or in pursuit of game would be conducted without the "correct" ceremonies.

Traditionally, Ojibway history and heritage were taught by the elders and others to the rest of the Ojibway clan. It was during these lessons that youths came to learn about the Manitous—their origin; presence; dwelling places; services and purposes; and kinship with all living beings, including plants, Mother Earth, animals and human beings. The Manitous were as much a part of reality as were trees, valleys, hills and winds. It was during these sessions that young people learned that Kitchi-Manitou infused everything and everyone with Manitou-like attributes and principles, which imparted growth, heal-

Through the centuries the Ojibway have lived a simple existence meeting their basic material needs. Many Natives believe it is because of this simplicity that their spiritual life is so rich. The dreamcatcher perfectly symbolizes the perfect unity between the Ojibway's rich spiritual life and their simple view of existence.

ing, character, individuality and identity. In traditional Ojibway culture, every person had a guardian manitou who provided protection in battle, success in hunting and identity within the group.

Beneficent spirits or manitous, such as the sun, moon, four winds, thunder beings and Grandfather Bear, were propitiated through prayer and tobacco offerings. These things were part of everyday life to the Ojibway and could not be separated from it. As well, particular care was directed to the placating of various malevolent spirits, such as the Weendigoes, the Giant Cannibals and the Matchi-auwishuk, the Evil ones. These were man-hunting manitous that preyed upon evil-doing humans, as well as those who gave in to excesses. The threat of the Weendigoes and Matchi-auwishuk was usually enough to bring about compliance with the perceived laws and established customs of the Ojibway clan. Except for these two malevolent spirits, there was nothing to fear of the manitous. It was, nevertheless, deemed prudent to court them with deference and offerings. Both sets of behavior were directed to the well-being of the entire community.

Of great personal concern and religious power was the acquisition of a guardian spirit, most often appearing during an individual's solitary vision quest, who could be called upon for guidance and protection. Dreams were regarded as revelations of the utmost importance, particularly the dreams and predictions of the priest or prophet,

who accompanied the warriors, and who was entrusted with the sacred sack of medicine. All dreams were reviewed for significance in predicting future events, acquiring power or foretelling the locations of game.

The dream state was often induced by fasting, isolation or meditation. It was the belief of the Ojibway that by possessing some representation of a dream subject one could at any time secure its protection, guidance and assistance. This belief was centered upon the fact that the Ojibway believed that the essence of an individual or of a "spirit" dwells in its picture or other representation. The dream representation could be made into an object or outlined as a picture and could be either an exact representation or an article or outline suggesting a peculiarity of the dream. The representation was often of the subject of the dream and rarely of the nature of the dream.

Stone was favored for dream representations because of its enduring properties. An older Ojibway man once told anthropologist Frances Densmore (1867-1957), "A picture can be destroyed, but stone endures, so it is good that a man have the subject of his dream carved in a stone pipe that can be buried with him. Many of his possessions are left to his friends, but the sign of the dream should not be taken from him."

Protective charms could be either direct representations or symbolic representations of dreams. The possession of a woven yard cord, for example, with the color white woven into it, when tied around the waist of a woman who had dreamed of a safe trip on a large lake, was believed to provide protection to her when traveling. A husband who dreamed of a bear when he was young could strengthen his very ill wife by spreading a cloth with the image of a bear over her and later hanging it by her head as she was getting stronger. A man who had dreamed of a rainbow, thunder bird, lightning and the earth (indicated by a circle) painted it on a blanket and wore it around his back and fastened across his chest for everyone to see, and a man who dreamed of an unusually shaped knife made one and carried it with him into battle.

At an early age, children were instructed to remember their dreams and given basic instruction in what they might mean. To answer group or individual concerns, a person recognized as having greater spiritual power often called upon his spirit helpers in what is known as a shaking tent performance.

Complementing the daily practice of this personal expression of spirituality, larger seasonal gatherings served to unify the dispersed groups through the more elaborate and complex religious expressions of the White Dog Feast, the Drum Dance and the practices of the Medaewaewin, or Medicine Lodge Society. The Medaewaewin, most often considered to be concerned primarily with health and healing,

Dreamcatchers are an important part of Ojibway spiritual life: they signify the Ojibway's close relationship with nature. Born of legend, the dreamcatcher continues to evolve, even to this day.

was a religious organization with mythic origins formulated around a hierarchical "shamanhood" or "priesthood," and was open to both men and women. Initiates passed through four grades or levels of instruction on the remedial powers and properties of different plants, on ritual knowledge and on sacred ceremonies in order to attain membership. A further four grades are optional in some lodges.

The Medicine Lodge Society still exists, and the Ojibway people continue to practice shamanic arts and natural healing. More and more Euro-Canadians have also turned towards naturopathy, herbalism and shamanism in a bid to both rescue humanity and attain the spiritual wholeness considered necessary for the healing process to take place. Just as the Ojibway recognize the essential union and crossing of paths between our conscious and unconscious self, so, too, does their method of healing recognize the intrinsic relationship between mind and body. People travel great distances to consult with a medicine man or a medicine woman. Just as the dreamcatcher is now widely popular and deeply appreciated for its natural estheticism and its power of psychic healing, so, too, the practices, ceremonies, rituals and cures of the Medaewaewin have not only been preserved but continue to flourish.

CHAPTER TWO

The Legend of the Dreamcatcher

BEFORE DRIFTING INTO DEEP SLEEP, WE REST OUR heads on our pillows with a silent prayer for sweet dreams— for ourselves and those we love. All parents wish they could guide the good dreams floating through our shared universe towards their infant as he or she lies blissfully asleep, and banish the bad ones. Waking up to a faint memory of a good dream, of a dream filled with love, light and good luck, signals the start of a good day. Being shaken out of sleep by a nightmare, a bad dream filled with evil spirits, self-doubt and sinister fears, does not bode well for the events of the coming day and is very unsettling to the spirit.

We spend nearly one-third of our lives inhabiting little known and less understood dream worlds. Yet all of our experiences and emotions—love and hatred, anticipation and fear, peacefulness and restlessness—are filtered through the two lenses of sleep and wakefulness. When we are awake, our open eyes are focused on the sights and subjects of the material world, on the real and concrete things that make up our day-to-day lives. But when our eyes close in sleep, our all-seeing vision is awakened, and we are invited into the world of our dreams, into an unconscious sphere far beyond the physical and the predictable.

It would seem but a thin line that divides the conscious and

Ojibway children were taught at an early age about the Ojibway relationship with the spirit world, with their manitous. Children were taught to honor and appease their manitous throughout life.

The dreamcatcher is made of all natural-materials. Wood that is pliable and easy to bend is chosen for the frame, and often deer, or other animal, sinew is used to "spin" the web inside the hoop. The natural material are representations of the Four Elements, and an integral part of Ojibway Society.

unconscious levels of the human psyche. For centuries, Europeans have wished to see man's unconscious drives subordinated to tangible and scientifically measurable concepts, easily understood and denuded of mystery. Even when haunted by dreams and altered psychic states, there was a desire to reduce all human experience to a collective reality and to order all human activity according to a strict set of morals and social mores. Historically, in Western culture, dreams and dream visions were legitimately explored only through art and literature. When Europeans first encountered cultures that approached the worlds of reality and imagination in another fashion, they derided these "outsiders" as primitives or savages, and condemned their religious beliefs for being pagan and anti-Christian. It was not until the end of the 19th century that Europeans began to confront their own dreams head on, and to read their dreams as coded messages dispatched from the illogical but nevertheless vital energies of the inner self to the rational and methodical outer being. Thanks in large part to the ground-breaking work of Sigmund Freud, Carl Jung and other pioneering psychologists, we have gradually come to accept that an essential relationship does indeed exist between our conscious and unconscious selves.

More than ever before, we are careful to remember our dreams,

Since the first dreamcatcher was made, dreamcatchers have undergone many rebirths. Today, dream-catchers such as this one are complex and vibrant with color. However, they still maintain the idea of simplicity and unity with the natural world.

to allow our unconscious to speak, and speak it does, loud and clear, to our conscious selves. Through personal dream journals, dream analysis, and even by talking to our loved ones about the tales and lessons we learned in the night, we are just as absorbed by our dreams during our waking hours as we are when we are asleep. For centuries, long before the emergence of dream therapy and psychoanalysis in Europe, the Ojibway people gave, and continue to give, high priority to the revelations of their dream state. The Ojibway order their existence according to their belief in the sometimes parallel, but more often intersecting, realms of physical reality and dream imagination. According to long-held Ojibway beliefs, the human self is divided between four states of existence: the body, the aura, the ego-soul. which leaves the body at death, and the free or shadow-soul, which is considered the part that comes alive in dreams.

For the Ojibway people, dreams are extremely important. They are visions of the spirit world and the means for acquiring spiritual power, and it is the message in a dream that determines everything from a child's name to the life-course a young adult will follow. However, it should be noted that for the Ojibway, dream experiences are not derived from the self, but rather are derived from external sources. Good dreams are, therefore, a true blessing. The dreamcatcher

Nearly one-third of our lives is spent inhabiting the dream world. The Ojibway believe that while we sleep, our all-seeing vision is awakened, and we are admitted into the world of dreams.

serves throughout one's life as an invitation for good dreams to come rest with the sleeper, as well as a fortification against nightmares and evil spirits.

In Ojibway tradition, mothers and grandmothers netted tiny circular cobweb-like charms from willow and sinew; these were not meant to last. They were intended to protect newborn babies from "everything evil as a spider's web catches and holds everything that comes in contact with it."[4] Evil in this context refers to colds, illness, bad spirits and malevolent powers. It is traditional to put a feather in the center of the child's dreamcatcher. The feather represents breath, or air, which is essential for life. A baby watching the air playing with the feather on the cradleboard was entertained while also being given a lesson on the importance of good air. This lesson comes forward in the way that the feather of the owl is kept for wisdom (a woman's feather) and the eagle feather is kept for courage (a man's feather). This is not to say that the use of each is restricted to gender, but that in using the feather in the dreamcatcher one is demonstrating awareness of the gender properties being invoked. Indian people, in general, are very specific about gender roles and identity. The woven dreamcatchers of adults do not use feathers at all.

In time, the willow of the child's dreamcatcher dries out and

The Ojibway have always ascribed special significance to the revelations of the dream state. They believe the physical reality and the dream reality to be two parts of one whole, neither more significant than the other. To the Ojibway, then, any kind of talisman related to the dream state, such as a dreamcatcher, was an important part of their culture.

the tension of the sinew collapses the dreamcatcher itself. This eventual collapse is intended; it symbolizes the temporariness of youth.

With the infant thus protected from invisible and negative forces, the child was able to grow into a competent, productive adult capable of providing for herself or himself as well as for the entire group. Thus, as an efficacious defense mechanism, these netted baby charms serve as a tangible metaphor of protection and provision, purposes which do not disappear after the child matures into an adult. Now marketed as dreamcatchers, these objects continue to provide lifelong protection for an individual.

The beauty of the dreamcatcher as an object is in its symmetry and its natural accents. For generations, the dreamcatcher has been crafted by making a hoop out of fresh wood, and then weaving a web inside the circle using deer sinew or colored thread. Careful attention is paid to leaving a hole in the middle of the web—if this is neglected, the healthy dreams cannot find their way through to the dreamer. Good dreams are also helped into the sleeper's dream world by feathers and colored beads that are attached at the bottom of the web. The feathers also represent air and breath, as good air is essential for the newborn child. The good dreams, which are instructive and intelligent,

The Ojibway believe dreams to be both visions of the spirit world and the means of acquiring spiritual power. This Ojibway dreamcatcher, made of willow and sinew, is meant for children. The feather in the center represents breath or air, which is essential for life.

will have no difficulty in finding the passage through. Only the bad dreams (bawedjigewin), which are dangerous and stupid, will get tangled in the web. As the legend goes, at the first light of dawn the bad dreams are consumed by fiery light and disappear from the face of the earth, while the good dreams have already had their effect and will allow the sleeper to awaken to a bright day full of hope.

There are many legends about the origins of the dreamcatcher, and many stories that explain how and why the first dreamcatcher was made.

The most popular legend about the dreamcatcher's origins features the grandmother and the spider. Once upon a time, long ago, the spider was silently spinning her web near the bed of N'okomiss, the grandmother. Day after day, the spider spun its glistening web while the grandmother looked on in appreciation. One day, as she was busy watching the natural miracle of the spider's design, N'okomiss's grandson intruded upon the scene. In his childish curiosity and mischievousness, the grandson lunged towards the spider and lifted his moccasin to squash the animal. As he raised his improvised weapon, N'okomiss yelled: "No, grandson, do not hurt the spider." Taken aback by his grandmother's reprimand, the grandson asked N'okomiss why she was protecting the spinning insect. She did not respond, but only smiled knowingly.

For the Ojibway, it is the messages in dreams, which are believed to originate not with the self but with external sources, that determine everything from a child's name to the life course a young adult will follow.

When the grandson left the sleeping quarters, the spider found its voice and spoke to the grandmother. The spider was grateful to N'okomiss for saving its life, and wished to return the gesture of protection and life-giving. The spider said: "For many days now you have been observing me as I wove my web, and you have admired my work. In return for your generosity, I would like to offer you a gift."

As night fell, the spider began to craft its web in the window of N'okomiss's wigwam, and instructed the grandmother to watch carefully how the web was woven. "Do you see how I weave? Watch and learn. From now on, in each web you weave you will be able to capture the bad dreams as they make their attempt to enter through your window. Only the good dreams will go forward through the small hole. This is my eternal gift to you."

In this legend it is the grandmother who brings the protection of the dreamcatcher to her extended family. As an elder of the community, she has the wisdom to respect all living things, all that has been created by the great Mother Earth. In her understanding of the co-dependence between human and animal spirits, N'okomiss knows intuitively that only good can come from the animals around her. Although it is the child who was about to commit the evil deed of murder, it is also the child who will be instructed against future fool-

This painting by Brad Kavanaugh depicts one of the many legends about the origin of the dreamcatcher: the legend of N'okomiss, the grandmother, and Asibikaashi, the Spider. In honor of the origin of the dreamcatcher, the number of points where the web connects to the hoop numbers eight, for Spider's eight legs. The eagle represents courage.

hardy acts by the powerful messages that will reach him in his dreams.

The emblematic role and life-saving capabilities of the spider in the legend of the dreamcatcher can be traced even farther back in Ojibway mythology. According to another Ojibway myth, there was a time long ago when the people were starving. Although there was an abundance of food, all the meat the hunters caught and trapped was fast rendered inedible by a flying pest who poisoned their provisions. There came to their rescue a six-legged insect who learned to weave a net that trapped the decay-producing flies. As a reward for its work, this insect was given an additional two legs as well as a new name, "Net Maker." In other Native stories, the Net Maker was often called Grandmother Spider or Spider Woman.

The legend of the grandmother and the spider suggests Ojibway women's unique ability for craft and beadwork. In the gendered division of labor in traditional Ojibway society, it was the women who were responsible for weaving and spinning. Women fabricated all sorts of netting: they made snares and fish and beaver nets; they wove the inner surface of snow shoes; and it was a female speciality to bead and lace the moss bags in which newborn children were ensconced. The need to have good feelings when one is working one's craft continues to this day. The Ojibway believe their crafts are a gift of beauty from the spirits.

Another legend about the origin of the dreamcatcher recounts the tale of Spider Woman, Asibikaashi, and the Manitou spirit, Nana'b'oozoo. Many of the elements in the story of the spider and N'okomiss are also present here. Long ago, when the world was young, the entire Ojibway people lived together on Turtle Island. The island was under cover of darkness, and it was Asibikaashi (Spider Woman) who came to Nana'b'oozoo's aid in his quest to restore the sun (giizis) to the people. To this day, Asibikaashi builds her distinctive lodge before sunrise, and at the break of dawn all glory in her webbed creation as the sun makes it shine brilliantly. If you are awake at dawn, as you should be, you can look for her lodge and see the miracle of how Asibikaashi captured the sunrise as the light sparkles on the dew that is gathered there.

Once the land was again flooded by light, the Ojibway scattered to the four corners of the earth to fulfill a prophecy, and Asibikaashi found it impossible to protect all her people in their distant lands. Unable to be by the bedside of each child as he or she awoke, Asibikaashi instructed the grandmothers (N'okomiss), mothers and sisters to take up the practice of weaving the magical webs for the new babies using willow hoops and sinew or cordage made from plants, which they found in their new homelands. The women had to make the dreamcatcher in the shape of the circle to represent the journey the sun makes across the sky every day.

In honor of the role that Spider Woman played in restoring light to the Ojibway people, children were warned never to harm or fear spiders but to honor, respect and protect them. As a reminder of the magical powers of the Asibikaashi, the web on the dreamcatcher was woven around eight points, the eight legs of the spider.

There is yet another legend about the origin of the dream-catcher. This one differs from the first two by suggesting that the originator was male, and that the spider spirit was far from benign. Again, we start near the beginning of time, when human and animal spirits understood one another, and when the spider could perform as a man.

Many generations ago, an elder spiritual leader ventured high upon a mountaintop and there had a vision. In the vision the spirit Iktomi, the great trickster and teacher of wisdom, came to the elder in the form of a spider. They spoke together in a sacred language different from that of the Ojibway people. As Iktomi spoke, he grasped the old man's willow hoop, which was covered with horsehair, feathers, beads and offerings to the spirits. Upon this hoop Iktomi began to spin a web.

The wise Iktomi spoke to the elder about the origins of the

The dreamcatcher is believed to serve throughout one's life as an invitation for good dreams to come rest with the sleeper, and as a fortification against nightmares and evil spirits.

world and the cycle of life, and emphasized the important role the old people play in caring for the very young. He uttered many warnings about the evil forces that confront humans as they go through their lives, and the necessity to steer clear of what is menacing and to take the right road. He told the elder how evil forces went against the forces of natural harmony. Throughout his long speech, Iktomi never stopped weaving his web.

Once the spider finished delivering his lesson, he handed his completed web to the elder and gave the following advice: "The web is a perfect circle with a hole in the center. Use the web to help your people reach their goals, making good use of their ideas, dreams and visions. If you believe in the great spirit, the web will catch your bad thoughts, and the good ones will go through the hole." The elder descended the mountain to return to his people, and with him he brought the first dreamcatcher.

In another myth, again taking place a time long ago, the Ojibway were already the great tribe of the Great Lakes region. However, it was a time of suffering, for the people were plagued by nightmares and dared not sleep. Not one of the elders had the wisdom to unravel the mystery of the nightmares plaguing their community, and so a council was convened of all the band's elders and medicine

Woven dreamcatchers, such as this one, are made for adults. The woven fiber is made up to reflect adult dreams. The use of gem stones was not something done in the old dreamcatchers. Today, the use of four gem stones represents the Four Directions.

men. Together they hoped to be able to find a cure for the people's troubled souls. During the conference, one of the elders had a vision in which he saw a thin wooden hoop decorated with feathers and beads, and what appeared to be a spider's web with a small hole in the center. The elder shared his vision with the people, and all took it to be an omen and set themselves to creating the object seen in the dream. Believing that dreams float continuously through the air in search of their final destination, the elders decided to hang their new creation over the sleeping child.

These are just some of the legends about the origin of the dreamcatcher. With so many accounts about its origin, we might be tempted to ask which is the authentic one. It is important to remember that, unlike the stories of the Judeo-Christian Bible, the Ojibway teachings were passed down orally; myths were never written down or codified. As Ojibway stories expand and change with each retelling, so there may be other versions of the same myth. If storytellers varied in their narrations, it was a question of their own personal style; what was, and is, important is the consistency of the message within each story. Given that the Ojibway people were dispersed over many territories, and that each community had its own storytellers and wise elders, it is hardly surprising that there should be more than one account of

The beauty of the dreamcatcher as an object is in its natural symmetry and its natural accents. The hoop is often made of fresh wood, and a web is woven inside the circle using deer sinew or colored thread. Careful attention is paid to leaving a hole in the middle of the web; if this is neglected, the healthy dreams cannot find their way through to the sleeper.

the first dreamcatcher. Today, the Ojibway's territory extends east to west from Lake Ontario to Lake Winnipeg (and including parts of Quebec), and north and south from the Severn River Basin to Minnesota, Wisconsin and Michigan. Further, they tend to be divided into four groups: the Southeastern, Southwestern, Northern (or Saulteux) and Plains (or Bungi) Ojibway.

While certain differences can be observed between the many stories, it is important to focus on their common points. What aspects do all these legends share? What elements of design and craft are essential in making the dreamcatcher effective?

Without exception, all these legends place emphasis on the importance of dreaming and the close relationship between spiritual life, which flourishes in the nocturnal world, and the protection of dream spirits during wakefulness. It is said that the Ojibway people learn a great deal from their dreams—where they first encounter the guardian spirit who will stay by their side all their lives—and that good dreaming is essential before anyone undertakes an important journey. Each legend also highlights the core beliefs of the Ojibway about the world of the supernatural. In the Ojibway world view, the natural and supernatural realms are continuous rather than disjointed, and the Manitou (other-than-human spirits) serve as a bridge between these two ways of perceiving reality.

What elements of design are common to all dreamcatchers? It may seem that there are as many ways to make a dreamcatcher as there are individuals for whom they are made. However, there are certain hard-and-fast rules in the production of the charms, and certain limits to the healing benefits that may be reaped from dreamcatchers. Some clues to these applications and restrictions can be gleaned from the account left by noted American ethnographer Frances Densmore (1867-1957), who dedicated her life's work to the study of American Indian music and culture. She first came into contact with the Ojibway on a trip to Port Arthur (now Thunder Bay), Ontario, in 1901, and set out to document and preserve what she believed was a "disappearing Indian culture." Among those bands she lived with, and studied in detail, during her long and distinguished career were the Ojibway at Grand Marais and at Grand Portage. Densmore was able to observe many of the customs and practices of the Ojibway people, and one of her consuming interests was Ojibway attitudes towards children and family.

Densmore documented the protective charms the Ojibway valued and considered sacred. Although she never identified these charms as dreamcatchers, she did write in detail about the uses and specifications of those protective articles made for infants. She described:

spiderwebs hung on the hoop of a cradle board. These articles consisted of wooden hoops about 3½ inches in diameter filled with an imitation of a spider's web made of fine yarn, usually dyed red. In old times this netting was made of nettle fibre. Two spider webs were usually hung on the hoop, and it was said that they caught any harm that might be in the air as a spider's web catches and holds whatever comes in contact with it.[5]

There are certain things we can know for certain about the dimensions and significance of the dreamcatcher's elements. The first dreamcatchers were, without exception, circular. The spherical shape is a reflection of the Sacred Hoop, the Great Circle of Life, of which we are all part. The unbroken strand of the web/sinew is symbolic of eternity, and of the life cycle that is continuously replenished and never-ending. The dreamcatcher must be made only of natural fibers and earthen articles, and this stems from the fact that it represents the four elements. Earth is symbolized by the wooden hoop and the mineral beads of sand, rock and clay. Air is symbolized by the feather as it sways ever so lightly in the breeze. Fire is essential if the dreamcatcher is going to fulfill its promise of destroying the bad dreams: the nightmares that have been tangled in the web are consumed by the sun's first rays every morning. Water is necessary for making pliable and manageable all the materials that are used to make the dreamcatcher: softening the deer hide, nourishing the fresh wood and allowing all living things to exist.

The Ojibway are very precise about the size and diameter of the dreamcatcher, and those that exceed this size can be considered beyond the scope of the tradition. The different natural elements—stones, feathers, parts of animals—that are added to the dreamcatcher each have their own significance and reflect the individual gifts, gender properties and special capacities of the person for whom it was made. For instance, certain parts of animals represent supernatural energies; the feather of the owl is used for wisdom (female), and the feather of the eagle represents courage (male).

The number of points from which every thread of the dreamcatcher is woven is far from arbitrary. While the Ojibway story of Spider Woman suggests that the web should be woven around eight points in remembrance of the spider's gift, it is often suggested that the dreamcatcher should have seven points around its diameter. These seven points represent the seven grandfathers, or the seven prophecies. There are also other numerologically significant combinations: a dreamcatcher may have thirteen points to signify the thirteen moons, or twenty-eight for the lunar month.

The Ojibway dreamcatcher is much more than a child's plaything or a decorative object. Born in legend, it is a constant reminder of universal flux, our mortality and the delicate harmony of the natural environment. The dreamcatcher is but a see-through curtain between the material and supernatural realms, and all good spirits are intelligent enough to float through this light veil and bless us by animating our dreams.

CHAPTER THREE

Dreamcatchers and Children

IN OJIBWAY CULTURE, AS IN MANY OTHERS, children are encouraged to play and share with their brothers and sisters, listen to the great and heroic stories passed down from their ancestors and, gradually, find their way to the roles they will fulfill as adults. The dreamcatcher, the Ojibway infants' very first toy, embodies parents' deepest hopes for their children's spiritual well-being: that they should be visited by only good dreams, and shielded from the small spirits or Manitous who would invade their nocturnal wanderings.

Children's dreamcatchers are made of very fragile material and are not meant to last; such is the nature of childhood itself. Crafted from delicate willow and sinew, children's dreamcatchers always have a feather at the center. As the wide-eyed infant watches how the air makes the feather sway back and forth, he or she catches a first glimpse not just of the wondrous play of nature, but of life's invisible essence made visible. In the past, the feathers that were used were those of the birds the Ojibway people held sacred: the owl's plume might be attached as a gift of wisdom, while the eagle's feather symbolized courage. In our own time, many laws have been passed by both the Canadian and the American governments forbidding the use of the

Good dreams are also helped into the sleeper's dream world by feathers or colored beads, attached at the bottom of the web. The good dreams, which are instructive and intelligent, have no difficulty finding passage through the center of the web.

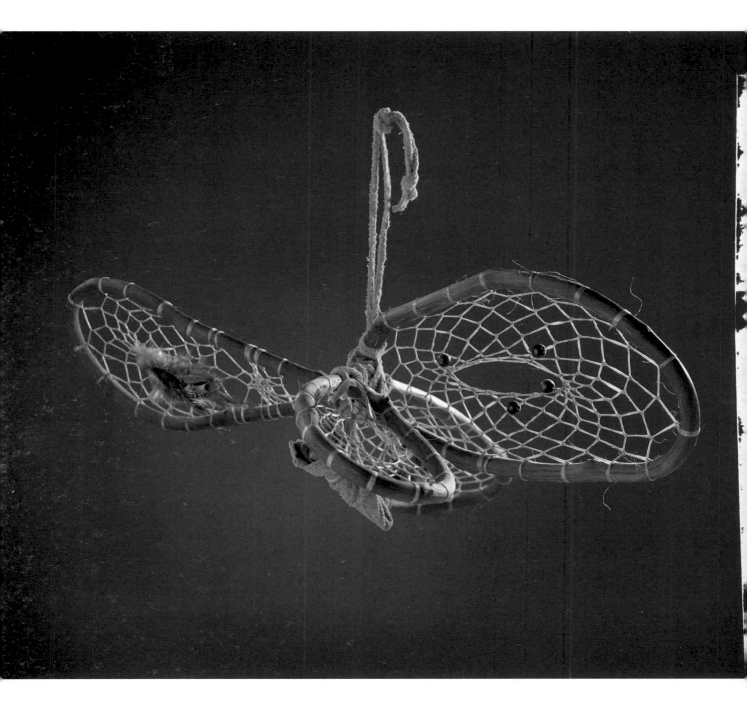

This dreamcatcher, made in a tear-drop shape, has four arms pointing into the Four Directions: North, South, East and West. The number four is sacred and figures prominently in Ojibway culture, religion, prophecies and oral traditions. Both spiritual and physical duality are represented in the Four Directions.

feathers of birds in danger of extinction. In place of the feathers of their sacred birds, Native North American artisans have begun to attach symbolic gem stones to their dreamcatchers.

When anthropologist Frances Densmore was living among the Ojibway at the beginning of the 20th century, she dedicated a great deal of attention to the ways in which Ojibway care for their infants. She observed that they tended to have small families of two or three children. The Ojibway mother was very attached to her newborn infant, and preferred to keep the baby with her at all times, leading Densmore to surmise that "the daily relation between mother and child was closer than in the white race."[6] Other non-Native researchers later went as far as criticizing Ojibway parents for "coddling" and "spoiling" their young children. Earlier in our century, the Ojibway parent's nurturing and indulgent expressions of love somehow clashed with the Euro-Canadians' stricter and more remote approaches to bringing up children. Today, few would criticize Ojibway parents, or any other parent for that matter, for trying to surround their offspring with love, security and closeness.

Two things were prepared before the birth of a child. First, the women collected sphagnum-moss and the down of cattail rushes, which they dried. They stuffed these natural insulators into sacs, and the newborn infant spent its first weeks cocooned in soft warmth.

An Ojibway mother and her child in the distinctive Ojibway cradle board, tikinagan. The tikinagan was usually made by either the father or the grandfather before the child was born. The mother would carry the child in the tikinagan upon her back at all times.

Second, before the child was born, either the father or the grandfather constructed and decorated the distinctive cradle board (tikinagan). This was a board measuring approximately 24 inches in length, with a curved piece of wood attached to the bottom that confined the baby's feet, and a hoop at right angles above the other end to protect the infant's head. The decorated covering that was stitched onto the frame was crafted by the infant's mother or grandmother. During each of these complementary creative processes, ancient songs were sung. Together the parents provided both physical and spiritual security and support for the growing infant. The mother would then wear the cradle board on her back, either by securing it much like we would wear a knapsack, or by hanging the board from her forehead by a strong piece of leather. The straps of the cradle board were adorned with elaborate bead and quill work, and it was from the upper bracket of the cradle board that the dreamcatcher and other trinkets were suspended. Consequently, a child's first bed was more than a practical crib—it was also a true work of art.

For the first two years of life, the cradle board was used as the child's bed, play pen and seat during transport, although after the first year the child was more and more frequently left to roam and discover the wonders of the physical world beyond. Ojibway mothers nursed their children until they were about two years old, some as long as

An original Ojibway tikinagan. This board usually measured approximately 24 inches in length, with a curved piece of wood attached to the bottom that confined the baby's feet, and a hoop at right angles above the other end to protect the infant's head. Often a dreamcatcher would be placed at the top to protect the child as it lay sleeping, as well as to amuse it while it was awake.

three or four years. Although lactation was more prolonged than in most European families, the Ojibway child was introduced to solid foods within the first year, such as porridge and fish roe, which was prepared like oatmeal.

It was not customary for parents to have a name ready when their child was born. Indeed, it was not the parents but a grandfather or even a designated "namer" (like a godparent) from outside the immediate family who was given the honorable task of naming the child. A child's name usually emerged from one of the namer's dreams. The namer bestowed more than a name on the newborn; he or she also transmitted the benefit and spiritual protection that he or she derived from the dream. All rejoiced upon the naming of the child, and the event was followed by a small ceremony and a feast.

The Ojibway child's play area was filled with many exciting and educational toys. Densmore described three sorts of charms hung on the cradle board and invested with spiritual meaning: the baby's umbilical cord, at least one net charm and other charms designed to ensure that a boy became a good hunter and a girl a good producer. So, for example, an infant boy might have a tiny bow, or the feet and hind legs of a fetal deer or moose. Infant girls' charms might include shells, beads or strips of cloth. There were also gifts offered to the child by the person who named the baby. The umbilical cord that had united

According to Ojibway legend, at the first light of dawn the bad dreams, caught in the web, are consumed by fiery light and disappear from the face of the earth, while the good dreams have already had their effect and will allow the sleeper to awaken to a bright day full of hope.

mother and child was preserved and kept in a durable case. Some say that this charm had the mystical effect of securing wisdom, while others claim that if the individual ever lost the umbilical charm they would spend their life in a fruitless search for something.

Babies were given rattles (shishikuan) that could be made from bear skin and carved wood. Little girls "played house," and enjoyed playing with dolls, which could be made out of either wood, sweet grass or cloth. Since it was assumed Ojibway society was not based on the ownership of private property but on deep respect for the natural environment that provided varied forms of sustenance and shelter in every season, Ojibway children were initiated early on into the practice of sharing their toys with family and friends. Ojibway children played the bowl game, archery, ring and toss, and, when they were older, lacrosse. (Lacrosse actually originated among the eastern tribes of the Ojibway, and it is now Canada's official national sport!)

While men and women labored together and worked in close co-operation, when approaching adolescence, boys and girls ceased playing together and began to learn the main skills appropriate to their gender. Roles according to sex, however, were not rigidly followed. For the most part, it was circumstance that dictated what men or women were to do when they were alone. Boys were trained to become skilled hunters and fishermen, and young women were trained in the arts of

cooking, sewing and mothering. Despite the traditional communal spirit and mode of life, however, the Ojibway people maintained the importance of individuality and personal independence on the premise that the more self-reliant and free the individual, the stronger and better the well-being of the community. The community was best served, naturally, by men and women who had been taught resourcefulness and had become independent masters of their own time, space and spirit, equals among themselves in the community. The roles of adulthood were imposed early—women might marry when they were fourteen or fifteen, and men when nineteen or twenty. This was all the more reason for the Ojibway child to be indulged during their early years.

Progress through each of life's stages was marked by ceremonies and rites. The infant was introduced into the band by the naming ceremony. There was a celebration when a boy killed his first prey, even if it was only a small animal. Boys and girls both embarked on a Dream Quest and fast in youth, during which they would discover the guardian spirits who would protect them throughout their lives. In order to take a woman in matrimony, a young man had first to adhere to certain customs. The young man approached the family of his intended bride by offering them an animal he had hunted as a sign of his sincerity and his ability to be a good provider. After the girl's father accepted that the couple should be united, the new husband was required to hunt with the bride's family during the first year, and the fruits of his labors belonged to his father- and mother-in-law. Every autumn the people gathered for the Festival of the Dead, and here they burnt food for the spirits of their loved ones who had passed on.

Ojibway wisdom, learning and customs were imparted to the most innocent by the most experienced. While parents educated their children in the practical knowledge needed for day-to-day survival, the elders informed children about the values and age-old insights of the people through storytelling, parables and fables, and by teaching them the arts of ceremonial songs and dances. In most Ojibway stories, it is N'okomiss, the grandmother, who serves as the narrator.

The principal teaching aid of the Ojibway people was the story, and for every event in their long history, for every belief about human and animal spirits, there was a fable. Storytelling was usually conducted during the long winter months, when children and adults would gather round their elders and see opened before them the heroic and adventurous lives and fates of both their guardian spirits and their menacing adversaries. For those youngsters who showed special gifts of learning, or who were identified as possessing superior strength of character and open-mindedness, this informal education was often followed by a more formal one. These youths were taken to see the

In one of the many popular legends regarding the origin of the dreamcatcher, an elder had a vision in which he saw a thin wooden hoop decorated with feathers and beads and what appeared to be a spider's web. The elder shared his vision with the other people, who took it to be an omen and set themselves to creating the object seen in the dream.

teaching rocks (kikiinoomaukae-assin). The "Rocks that Teach" are the petroglyphs pecked into crystalline limestone near Peterborough, Ontario. Roughly dated to between 500 and 1000 years old, the nearly 900 glyphs were used by many groups as teaching rocks to instruct their youth. Areas believed to be sites of spiritual contact were used as locations for Vision Quests. As previous visions were often made tangible in pictographs and/or petroglyphs, these areas were considered numinous and hence significant for a youth's quest. Here the elders would guide them through the stories represented by the petroglyphs and on birchbark scrolls. These specially selected children were the ones being tutored in the art of storytelling and teaching, so that one day, when they became adults, they too would have the young gather around them during the long evenings of winter to hear the fables and history of their people.

The Ojibway people continue to be prolific and gifted story-tellers. Aside from those legends that are inscribed for posterity upon the teaching rocks, their tradition is an oral one. Ojibway stories have developed over time, and in each generation they reflect the current concerns and experience of the people. Every legend, then, has undergone many retellings and many subtle recastings, as each storyteller adds the personal touch of his or her own creative vision. This is as true for the legends surrounding the dreamcatcher as for any other.

Without exception, all of the different legends surrounding the dreamcatcher place a great deal of emphasis on the importance of dreaming and the close relationship between spiritual life and the dream state. The manitou, which served as a bridge between these two worlds, were often paid homage to by burning tobacco or with other ancient ceremonies.

One of the many Ojibway legends that also touches on the same concept as the legend of the dreamcatcher is Norval Morrisseau's account about the Great Medicine Spider's gift to the Ojibway people. As the legend goes, centuries ago, the Great Medicine Spider appeared to the Ojibway people to teach them how to make a web that would protect them from evil forces, made from fine strips of untanned hide, commonly called babiche, or from sinew.

It is believed that if a sorcerer comes to harm the owner of the sacred net, his spirit body, or dream body, will be caught like a fly in this net and be devoured by the spider, and if that spirit body is caught his real body, including his spirit body, will die. Today these sacred nets can still be seen among the Ojibway, made of fine thread with small rattles tied on both sides.[7]

From childhood, the Ojibway people repeat the stories of their omnipresent Manitou—half-animal, half-human spirits who possess supernatural powers and transcendent wisdom. First among the Manitou is Kitchi-Manitou, also known as the Great Mystery. It was Kitchi-Manitou who, in fulfillment of a vision, created the world, created animal life and animal consciousness, separated the seasons and also created the other Manitous. Among the other Manitous who belong to the Ojibway pantheon of other-than-human beings are Geezhigo-Quae, or Sky Woman, the spirit of the heavens and the mother of the Anishinaubae people; Muzzu-Kummik-Quae, or Mother Earth, who is responsible for providing all humans with food and shelter, and can impart the power of healing; Kawawsind, or the Feared One, who was assassinated by the other Manitous for his evil deeds and who has come to represent bullying, abuse and victimization; and Pau-eehnse, the little Manitou who dwells on shores and beaches and will awake in the night in order to warn humans about the mermaids and mermen who haunt the waters. Of the Manitous best loved by children are the Maemaegawaehnssiwuk, or the little people, who have the appearance of miniature humans and are shaggy, hairy and mischievous. The Ojibway Manitou world is far from idyllic. It reflects both the potential and the shortcomings of the human animal, and serves as a parallel world from which warnings and prophecies can emerge.

In Ojibway mythology, it is in the fable of the union between Ae-pungishimook, the Manitou of the West and the symbol of old age and death, and the mortal Winonah that the equivalent of a "holy family" exists. Ae-pungishimook came upon Winonah while she was in the forest collecting berries, and temporarily separated from her party.

Here he took her, and ravished her, just as age always achieves violent conquest over youth. With her, he fathered four sons: Maudjee-kawiss, Pukawiss, Cheeby-aub-oozoo and Nana'b'oozoo. Each son was a demi-god, part human and part manitou.

Maudjee-kawiss was Winonah and the Manitou's first son. When Ae-pungishimook surreptitiously came back to the camp to take a look at his firstborn, he was pleased to see that his infant son was vigorous and full of unbridled energy. As he watched his son, he had a dream vision of Maudjee-kawiss, where he saw that the boy would grow into a great hunter, fisherman, trapper and defender of the nation. Maudjee-kawiss fulfilled his father's prophecy. He was the hunter and the warrior, and, through all his exploits in an adventurous life, symbolizes care, diligence and courage.

Winonah and Ae-pungishimook's second son was Pukawiss. He differed from his older brother in being neither serious nor practical, and from childhood he was fascinated by watching and observing the birds, animals and insects as they played in their unspoiled habitats. To his people, Pukawiss brought the joy of dance and music, humor and revelry, and the appreciation of fine dress and human-made arts. His Manitou father disapproved of his search for amusement and saw little point in his dedication to performance. Because his father forsook him in this way, Pukawiss is also known as the Disowned. Although his

The number of points from which every thread of the dreamcatcher is woven is far from arbitrary. While the legend of the Spider suggests the web should be woven around eight points, often seven points are used, representing the seven grandfathers or seven prophecies, or twenty-eight points may be used to represent the twenty-eight lunar months.

humorless and powerful father looked down on his second son, Pukawiss has a secure place in the hearts of the Ojibway people, who credit him with gracing them with their love for music, dance and colorful ceremony.

Ae-pungishimook and Winonah's third son was Cheeby-aub-oozoo, who, from childhood, had a special relationship to the spiritual and supernatural worlds. It was in a dream that this deep knowledge was revealed to Cheeby-aub-oozoo, and it became his life's work to teach his people the lesson that humankind and Manitou would henceforth communicate in the dream world. Although Cheeby-aub-oozoo had such deep insight and such spiritual power, he was not immune to human failings or the evil notion of pride. For instance, he could not ignore the taunt of his eldest brother, Maudjee-kawiss, who dared him to seek out and attempt to pacify Beboonikae, the northern-dwelling Manitou who was held responsible for winter hardship. Soon after embarking on his mission, his canoe tipped over and Cheeby-aub-oozoo lost his life in the treacherous waters. After he drowned in the lake, Cheeby-aub-oozoo rose again as a ghost, and he became known as the Chief of the Underworld. Among the gifts he bestowed upon the Ojibway people are poetry and spiritually purifying music and chants.

Winonah and Ae-pungishimook's fourth and last son was Nana'b'oozoo. Winonah died shortly after his birth, and his Manitou father never came to visit him when he was a child, so that his grandmother, N'okomiss, was solely responsible for his upbringing. Among the four brothers, he came closest to becoming a full-fledged Manitou, although his failings were frequently met by misfortune. The Ojibway people tell hundreds of stories about his misadventures, his impetuous acts and his disrespect for both his human and his supernatural families, as well as his profanation of ceremonies and customs. Nonetheless, Nana'b'oozoo is beloved among the people, as he represents to them the coexistence of good and evil drives in our human nature.

Nana'b'oozoo is also the patron Manitou of Ojibway children. Anishinaubae scholar and storyteller Basil Johnston tells us how Nana'b'oozoo was especially fond of children and sought always to restore their smiles, elicit their laughter and wipe away their tears and sorrows. As the legend goes, there was a time when the Ojibway children had no toys except sticks and stones, bark and ants and beetles. The infants in Nana'b'oozoo's village were suddenly stricken by a severe case of melancholy, to the point where they could no longer muster the playfulness to laugh. In their melancholy, the children also grew weak and prone to illness. The adults and community elders made every attempt to cheer them up, but to no avail. Basil Johnston tells us what happened next:

> As a last resort, the people in the village sent for Nana'b'oozoo, more out of desperation and for the sake of appearance than from a real belief that his "champion" could do anything.
>
> Nana'b'oozoo was no more successful than anybody else. Actually, he frightened the children even more, so they cried and screamed without let up until the people had to ask him to leave the children alone.
>
> To have failed, and worse, to have been asked to go away, wounded Nana'b'oozoo's pride.
>
> Unable to forget the children and their condition, Nana'b'oozoo made up his mind to speak directly to Kitchi-Manitou. For this purpose he went in search of the highest mountain in the land, from whose summit he hailed and cried out to the Creator.
>
> Kitchi-Manitou answered with a riddle, but Nana'b'oozoo could not decipher it. "Even stones have wings," Kitchi-Manitou said.
>
> Later, exasperated by his inability to solve the riddle,

Nana'b'oozoo took a handful of coloured pebbles and pitched them over his shoulder in frustration. In midair the pebbles turned into butterflies of every colour, shape, and size behind Nana'b'oozoo, who didn't notice the miracles.... Nana'b'oozoo was still nowhere near solving the riddle or finding something that would uplift the spirits of the children, when he decided to go home, empty-handed. Behind him followed the butterflies.

Children's eyes that had been dull and dim lit up, little arms that had been limp came to life, legs that had been wasted broke into a run, and faces that had been woebegone broke into smiles as the little boys and girls ran after these soft, small creatures that fluttered in the wind.

Since that day when Nana'b'oozoo returned from the west followed by these fragile creatures, butterflies have been the symbols of children's play and happiness. Our people called them *maemaegawauhnsswuk*, little feathers, kin to the people in the forest, the maemaegawaehnssiwuk, who appear only to children and sometimes play with them and care for them in the forest if they are lost.[8]

Just like the butterfly, the whimsical feather attached to the child's dreamcatcher entertains and brings sweet tidings to the Ojibway child. Through adventurous stories, the protective and loving instincts of parents, and sacred charms, the Ojibway have furnished a world for children where the young will always find nurture, education and safety. The dreamcatcher's protection is perhaps even more important for young adults, whose future will be determined by the visions and spirits who appear in their dreams.

CHAPTER FOUR

The Dream Quest

I N THE DREAM QUEST, THE RITE OF PASSAGE EMBARKED
upon by boys and girls on the threshold of adulthood, the child's
dream is transformed into a waking, visionary experience. Those
visions will serve not only to guide and instruct the quester on his or
her life course but also to establish the connections with the Manitou
spirits who will help in his or her adult life. The world that opens
up before the Native youth embarking upon his or her Dream Quest
is a transcendent world of profound realities and sacred symbols.
Indeed, it could be said that for the Ojibway, life does not begin so
much when a newborn baby enters the world, but, rather, when the
young soul is first awakened to dreams about his or her deeper con-
nection with the natural and supernatural forces that together govern
the universe.

Dreams, prophecies communicated through dreams and extra-
sensory contact with beings who flourish in the dream world are all
central themes in Ojibway legends. With some obvious parallels to the
stories of Creation in other religions, for the Ojibway it is Kitchi-
Manitou who, alone, created the world. What induced Kitchi-Manitou
to undertake such a magnificent task? He had a vision in which he saw,

*This dreamcatcher has thirteen moons,
representing the thirteen moons of Ojibway
culture. This dreamcatcher also incorporates megis
shells in its design. Megis shells play an important
part in Ojibway customs, oral traditions and
religion. According to Ojibway oral history, each
major stopping point during the Ojibway
migration from the St. Lawrence Seaway area
west to what is today northern Michigan,
northern Wisconsin, northern Minnesota,
southern Ontario and as far west as Manitoba
would be marked by the appearance of the Sacred
Megis Shell.*

smelled, tasted, touched and heard man, plants, animals and other
Manitous. In remembrance of the miracle of Creation, which originated in a dream, every member of the Ojibway nation must embark
on a Dream Quest in order to come into contact with his or her
guardian spirit or spirit helper. As the world was created in a dream
vision, so too the mature self comes to life in dreams. The contents of
the vision the youth has during the Dream Quest will determine his or
her personal mission in life. It is the adolescent's meeting with destiny,
the coming of age. More significantly, it establishes the all-important
bonds with the unseen reality; together they survive.

Only in the dream world can the Ojibway come into contact
and travel with their Manitou spirits. According to legend, it was
Cheeby-aub-oozoo, Winonah and Ae-pungishimook's third son, who
was the first man to commune with the Manitous. To emulate this
breakthrough in communication with the supernatural world, both
men and women ventured to a quiet and isolated spot that was known
to be visited by the Manitous. Once there, they waited for dreams and
visions to be visited upon them. The dreamer might have called to the
Manitous to come forward and grant him or her a wish. If the dream
seeker's petition was convincing enough, the Manitous were known to
appear and grant the favors requested. Gradually, the practice spread,
and it became customary for anyone who was planning a journey or

preparing a potent curative to call forth the Manitou by chanting and drumming. With the Manitou's blessing, the dreamer would be assured good luck and good speed.

In a turn of tragic irony, just as the vision of the world's glorious Creation first came in the form of a dream, so too did the prophecy of the white man's destruction and attempted annihilation of the Ojibway people and their spirit. As the legend goes, the tribal storyteller Daebaudijimoot was approached by Auttissookaunuk, the Muses, in a dream. In the vision that the Muses placed before the storyteller's dreaming eyes, there arose the image of a man who was white all over, and who had hair that grew from his arms, his legs, his chest, his back and his armpits. According to the premonition, traveling in large vessels many times the size of the birchbark canoe, these white men would come across the salty waters in great numbers. Daebaudijimoot's prophecy was very finely detailed and, in retrospect, lamentably accurate. In his dream he had seen that the following would transpire:

> In the beginning the first few to arrive will appear to be weak
> by virtue of their numbers, and they will look as if they are no
> more than harmless passersby, on their way to visit another
> people in another land, who need a little rest and direction

before they resume their journey. But in reality they will be spies for those in quest for land.[9]

Daebaudijimoot was given the ominous gift of sight deep into the future. He was also shown the devastating impact that the white man would have on the "original people's" ancestral lands:

> [O]ver the years the white people will take possession of all the rest and they will build immense villages upon them. Over the years the white people will prosper, and though the Anishinaubaek may forsake their own traditions to adopt the ways of the white people, it will do them little good. It will not be until our grandchildren and their grandchildren return to the ways of their ancestors that they will regain strength of spirit and heart.[10]

Although this dream told of sad events in the future of the Ojibway people, it is interesting to note how even this dark prophecy concluded with a message of hope and redemption.

In the past, every Ojibway youth sought assistance in life from spiritual beings through a Dream Quest. The end of childhood innocence was marked by a solitary journey into the forest in search of such a dream. For many days, the questers would refrain from food, drink and sleep until the moment when a vision appeared to them or they beheld dream visitors (pawaganak).

According to many observers, although girls were also encouraged to dream and listen to their dreams, greater importance was given to the Dream Quest the boys embarked on in puberty. Boys were between the ages of 10 and 14 when they went in search of their guardian spirits, their Manitous, or their spiritual grandfathers. Many customs surrounded the Dream Quest, and it was crucial to follow each ritual step with care for the quest to be successful.

In recent years, when noted ethnographer and scholar A. Irving Hallowell studied the customs of the Ojibway of Berens River, Manitoba, he took note of the following prescriptions and proscriptions imposed on the adolescent dream quester. The boy was led by his father or by his grandfather to a mountaintop. Here the boy prepared a rock platform for himself. He was forbidden to descend from the mountaintop for any purpose other than to take a drink of water.

The boy had to be sexually "pure" or the fast was useless. Even less intimate relations with girls or women were avoided immediately before or after the fast, which signalled both the psychological and social identification of boys with mature members

The first dreamcatchers were, without exception, circular. The spherical shape is a reflection of the Sacred Hoop, the Great Circle of Life, of which we are all part. The unbroken strand of the web/sinew is symbolic of eternity, and of the life cycle that is continuously replenished and never-ending.

of their own sex. For several days before departing the boy slept in the "cleanest" place in the dwelling, that is, towards the rear, the area reserved for the men…During the fasting period the boy's father or grandfather might sing and drum to communicate with his own other than human tutelaries and to invoke help on behalf of the dreamer.[11]

In his vision, the quester may interact with the sacred Manitou, or he may communicate with animals and other humans. In his heightened state of consciousness, the dreamer may even be metamorphosed into a Manitou. The youth's future life course was determined by the dream, and depending on which guardian spirit he acquired, he would always be protected, whether he became a hunter, a warrior or a shaman.

Whether it is a consequence of greater freedom being allowed to women in our day, or because Dream Quest practices differ between the dispersed Ojibway communities, today some Ojibway women also embark on a Dream Quest. The anthropologist Theresa S. Smith, who has conducted field work among the Anishnaabeg of Manitoulin Island, has encountered women who went on the Dream Quest and fast shortly after their first menstruation. Indeed, Manitoulin Island has a long history of Ojibway habitation, and on the White Fish

Reserve tourists can visit Dreamer's Rock, a site of pilgrimage and sacred significance. It was not long ago that the Ontario Historical Society placed a plaque on the site of Dreamer's Rock. One of Smith's consultants, Beth Southcott, felt it was unfortunate that the plaque describes the Ojibway youth's Dream Quest in the past tense, while "completely ignoring the contemporary procession of young painters which daily climbs through woodland trails and scales the smooth flanks of the summit for inspiration. The quest is continuous."[12]

The visions the adolescents receive during their Dream Quests are as different one from another as each person is unique. Although there is a great respect for individuality and the value of each dreamer's vision, some dreams are more important than others. Some dreams could be regarded as prophecies designed to warn the people as a whole, particularly those dreams that tell of a forthcoming victory or defeat in warfare. The recipient of such portentous dreams can often rise to a leadership position in a time of inter-tribal warfare or when the Ojibway are in conflict with the encroaching white man.

It is also considered essential that dreamers keep their dreams to themselves—a dream is a secret to be shared with nobody else. Just as a fortune teller will command you never to reveal your fortune to anyone else if you want it to come true, so the dream quester is to remain silent about their vision. In fact, it has been said that if the dreamer reveals the content of their formative dream to another person, they are in danger of losing the help, power and benefit that the dream visitor or guardian spirit had generously bestowed upon them. Throughout life, the dreamer is obliged to pay reverence to the guardian spirit who appears in their youthful vision. The dreamer has to show respect and fidelity, and present offerings, such as tobacco.

Although the content of the dream has to remain secret, the Ojibway do use the more prominent symbols of their dreams to adorn various personal articles. For example, the images from their dreams might be woven with beads into a pattern on a carrying sac or a mat, or these individualized symbols could be used to decorate the war shields used by the Plains Ojibway. The images that appear in dreams were once etched in rocks close to the sacred forested sites frequented by dream questers. On a nature walk through these enchanted forests, you may be lucky enough to come across one of these rocks yourself.

Dreams awaken the mind to the inter-dependence of the natural and supernatural worlds, and to the co-dependence between the body and the spirit. As a passage to maturity, adolescents are set upon their Dream Quest and begin to make their own decisions and set their own life course according to the vision that opens up before

The dreamcatcher must be made only of natural fibers and earthen articles, and this stems from the belief that it represents the four elements. Earth is symbolized by the wooden hoop and the mineral beads of sand, rock and clay. Air is symbolized by the feather as it sways in the breeze.

them. Dreams may bring good tidings, and dreams may also alert the dreamer to dangers ahead. Throughout life, prophetic dreams are sought before embarking on a new venture, a hazardous journey or a treatment of medicinal remedies for an illness. Central to the human experience, dreams reveal the richness of the human condition.

It is for all these reasons that the Ojibway dreamcatcher is such a symbolically charged and meaningful talisman. Whether it hangs over the child's cradle board to fend off the bad dreams, or is suspended above the adult's pillow as an invitation only to good thoughts and helpful spirits, the dreamcatcher plays an important part in a healthy spiritual life.

CHAPTER FIVE

Contemporary Issues

THE SPIRITUAL LEGACY OF DREAMCATCHERS

Nobody can escape dreams or live exclusively within the world of consciousness in the light of day. Few of us are blessed with the gifts that allow us to live without nightmares, periodic feelings of restlessness or gripping fear. Without exception, we must sleep and trust our own soul to deliver our mind and body to safety on the morning of each new day. As interpreted by those of West European origin and tradition, the never-ending interplay between the conscious self, the imagination and the unconscious self is the essence of the human spiritual condition. It is for these reasons that the Native North American dreamcatcher catches the imagination of so many people. For First Nations people themselves, the dreamcatcher is a sacred talisman that continues to work its magic. The Ojibway trust that Kitchi-Manitou will conduct them and watch over them and lead them through the night and into the next day. For others, the dreamcatcher has become a comforting and protective amulet against the bad thoughts and bad feelings that too often distract us from our search for inner harmony and natural balance.

Although the first known dreamcatchers were made by the Ojibway people, with the passage of time, dreamcatchers have become

The Ojibway are very precise about the diameter of the dreamcatcher, and those that exceed approximately 3.5 inches in diameter can be considered beyond the scope of the tradition. The different natural elements—stones, feathers, parts of animals—that are added to the dreamcatcher each have their own significance and reflect the individual gifts, gender properties and special capacities of the person for whom it was made.

Today dreamcatchers come in all shapes and sizes. This untraditional dreamcatcher is a glorious combination of the Ojibway's ability with beadwork and traditional dreamcatcher style. Ojibway women are known for their exquisite work with beads. They believe in the need to have good feelings when one is beading because these gifts of beauty are believed to come from the spirits.

part of many different Native cultures. Today, Cree, Oneida, Sioux and many other bands consider dreamcatchers to be part of their heritage, and an enduring symbol of their cultural life. With the increasing public interest in First Nations culture, Native arts and crafts, and aboriginal beliefs, institutions, perceptions, outlook and healing, dreamcatchers have also captured the imagination of people from diverse cultural backgrounds.

Today, dreamcatchers represent psychic healing and are used by children and adults alike as a shield against threatening nocturnal spirits. Native artisans continue to craft ever fresh versions of the dreamcatcher and offer their enchanting wares to a public that is captivated by the charm. The sale of dreamcatchers also provides an income, which is invaluable to many talented Native craftspeople who bend and weave their delicate materials to create these wondrous webs. The making of less elaborate dreamcatchers provides a pleasurable pastime for children, and by crafting the delightful suspended talisman, the young are introduced to an ancient world and an age-old set of beliefs.

The tradition of the dreamcatcher is forever evolving and modernizing. You can find many artists who will make you a dreamcatcher to meet your own specifications, reflect your personal imagery and symbols, or incorporate your own charms and heirlooms. Among the choices you will find are dreamcatchers in the traditional circular design, in the shape of a teardrop, a snow shoe or a heart, or made out

The dreamcatcher, the Ojibway infant's very first toy, embodies the parents' deepest hopes for their children's spiritual well-being: that they should be visited by only good dreams and shaded from the small spirits or Manitous who would invade their dream-state wanderings.

of three lengths of wood to form a triangle. Sizes range from the very small for earrings, pendants and key chains, to the traditional measurement of 3½ inches in diameter, to gigantic woven hoops that can be seen from a mile away. Many materials are used, including willow hoops, leather strips, mineral beads and real feathers; you will probably also come across dreamcatchers made out of human-made fibers, brass hoops, dyed feathers, brilliant acrylic beads and shimmering ribbons. Prices also vary depending on the intricacy of the craftsmanship and the reputation of the craftsperson. Some dreamcatchers may also be more expensive if precious stones or rare material are incorporated in the design.

Many of these contemporary trends could be considered unfaithful to the original purpose and sacred design of the Ojibway dreamcatcher. Some criticisms have been raised over the past few years that dreamcatchers exceeding a certain size do not conform with tradition. In 1995, for instance, a controversial debate raged on the NativeTech web site about the origins and present-day uses of dreamcatchers. One respondent was scandalized when he saw a dreamcatcher at a truck stop that was about six feet in diameter.

While there is much to be said for purity and remaining true to ancient custom, it could also be argued that by widening the applications and uses of the dreamcatcher, by sharing the dreamcatcher with all who are instinctively attracted by its beauty and its deeper meaning,

The world that opens up before the Native youth embarking upon his or her Dream Quest is a transcendent world of profound realities and sacred symbols. The dreamcatcher is the Native youth's first foray into this world.

it has become a living and familiar symbol of human striving for goodness and inner peace.

Similar to the Ojibway use of dreamcatchers, many cultures rely on certain practices and charms to ward off the effects of malevolent spirit forces, particularly when protecting an infant or child. Protection of the infant is paramount in those societies that depend upon an individual's contribution to the welfare of the group. For example, there is often a reliance on a charm used to protect against the Evil Eye, whether it be the Central American god's-eye pendant or the Middle Eastern Hand of Fatima. Similarly, in North Africa, the mother of a small child will place a piece of holy wood in her child's pillow to scare away mischievous night-time visitors. Each of these customs has arisen from specific cultural and religious contexts. However, over many centuries, they have become universal and part of our shared appreciation and apprehension of the power of the unknown. The Native American dreamcatcher can be compared to these charms and these customs, and it holds in common with many of these other sacred objects, legends and superstitious sayings the function of repelling evil and inviting good luck and good times.

Yet, even with their increasing popularity and commercialization, dreamcatchers are still considered to be gifts from the spirit world, and their creators take great pride in the intricate beauty of these artifacts and relish the spiritual aspects of their labors. It is still believed that power and knowledge come through dreams, and so the dreamcatcher continues to reinforce these beliefs.

The materials used for dreamcatchers differ according to the intended recipient. A child's dreamcatcher, for example, is made of fresh red willow, deer hide and a few beads and feathers. It is said that the deer hide has the power to take away sadness. Contemporary dreamcatchers for adults are made of more durable materials, and are meant to last a lifetime. While many artisans try to remain true to the specifications of the original dreamcatchers, are careful to make the charms to reflect sacred legends, and prefer to craft them in the natural settings and enchanted spots inhabited by ancestors and ancestral spirits, some radical changes have occurred in terms of where dreamcatchers are displayed and sold.

Where can you find dreamcatchers today? You can see them displayed in almost every gallery that specializes in Native art, or you can buy them in any shop that sells Native crafts. You can find them being sold by the people who have crafted them at outdoor arts and crafts fairs, or you can acquire them from street vendors. You can find them in the craft stores attached to many Native North American cultural foundations, community centers or museums. Wherever you go on your dreamcatcher quest, you will usually find attached to the charm a little descriptive card repeating the legend and purpose of the dreamcatcher. This is because the dreamcatcher's beauty lies as much in its intriguing symbolic meaning as in its esthetically pleasing appearance.

You may well come across advertisements for Native artisans who offer to make dreamcatchers especially for you, by using the articles, fibers, beads and feathers of your choice. Although it is traditional to use only natural materials, some artisans today will use acrylic beads, plastics and metallic hoops as well. As many people will tell you, when you are looking to purchase a dreamcatcher, try to find one that pleases you and reflects your personal imagery and intimate symbols. After all, the dreamcatcher is both a sacred charm that has evolved among the Ojibway people and an object representing the individual over whose bed it hangs. Also remember that no matter how lovely the dreamcatcher looks hanging from either a rear-view mirror, a doorway or a balcony, its true place is over a bed or in the window that opens upon the sleeper. No matter what its modern incarnations and decorative applications, the dreamcatcher will always be regarded as a shield against the bad dreams that float through our shared space in the collective unconscious, as well as an easy passage through which the good dreams may come.

Another place where you will come across many different versions of intricately woven dreamcatchers is on the world wide web! The electronic highway can take you to myriad destinations where dreamcatchers are exhibited and sold. The fact that so many forms and varieties of dreamcatchers can be found on the Internet is indicative of their popularity, their adaptability and their renewed significance.

Who makes dreamcatchers? Almost anyone can make a dream-catcher, either for their own personal use or as a gift for a child or a loved one. While authentic dreamcatchers are made by Native artisans who fully comprehend the legends and customs of their people, dreamcatchers have become so popular that you will find many craft manuals that will instruct you on how to make them. The materials needed can be purchased at almost any craft store in North America.

Materials for dreamcatchers can also be gathered in parks, in the woods and on the seashore. But beware what you pick up in the out-of-doors and then use in your dreamcatcher! In 1995, one partic-ular dreamcatcher became the subject of some controversy. In August of that year, national newspapers reported the story of Peg Bargon, a housewife and craftmaker from Monticello, Illinois, who made a home-made dreamcatcher to present as a gift to the First Lady, Hillary Rodham Clinton.

For many years, Bargon had been making dreamcatchers and selling them at a local arts and crafts mall. When Hillary Clinton vis-ited the University of Illinois in 1994, a Democratic party worker sug-gested to Mrs. Bargon that she offer one of her lovely creations to the First Lady. Bargon sent the dreamcatcher to Mrs. Clinton, and received a kind thank-you letter from the First Lady. Some time later, however, to Bargon's great surprise, her home was raided, her property ransacked and her craftmaking materials confiscated by agents from the U.S. Fish and Wildlife Service. She faced a large fine and the possibility of imprisonment because she had incorporated a feather from the American bald eagle in her dreamcatcher design. Reportedly, she was unaware that it was against the law to possess this majestic bird's feathers. Not only is the bald eagle America's national emblem, but it is a creature on the list of endangered species. It is stipulated in American law that to possess either eagle feathers or feathers of migratory birds with intent to sell carries a fine of up to $100,000 and a sentence of one year in jail. Like so many people who like to make dreamcatchers, Bargon told reporters that she customarily went on nature walks to find the materials she uses in her crafts, and she claimed that she had found this bald eagle feather on the ground in the zoo.[13] So, in choosing natural materials, be mindful of issues of local ecology.

Crossing cultural boundaries and continents, dreamcatchers continue to be made for children who suffer from nightmares. In January 1997, Susan Cockle, a Scottish-born child psychologist working in Edmonton, Alberta, made a very touching humanitarian gesture when she arranged for dreamcatchers to be sent to the traumatized survivors of the massacre in Dunblane, Scotland. Some 700 children from Dunblane Primary School witnessed the horrific scenes of March 13, 1996, when a mad gunman opened fire in a classroom and killed sixteen classmates. The children who witnessed this horrible event continued to suffer from nightmares for a long time after it. Included in the packages sent to the children through the Dunblane Healing Gift Project were items of therapeutic value: a sketch pad, crayons, a guardian angel pin, a feelings chart and a dreamcatcher. The dreamcatchers were made and then donated by a number of groups across Alberta and British Columbia, including the Edmonton Institution for Women, two First Nations schools and the Girl Guides and Pathfinders. Cockle was glad to find out that the dreamcatchers worked their magic, and among the many letters of thanks she received was one from a little girl who wrote that she had not had any nightmares since the night she hung the dreamcatcher in her bedroom window.[14]

Although in Ojibway legends net charms are made by the mother or the grandmother of a newborn infant, today, children are making dreamcatchers for themselves at school, in arts and crafts classes, and at home. In so doing one would hope that the legends of the Ojibway people will be carried on and will help to promote creativity and spirituality in all races. In addition, if the legend of the dreamcatcher continues to move throughout various cultures in this way, children will learn a great deal about the "original and first man" to inhabit the North American continent. As an expression of a curiosity and taste for the brilliantly colorful and playful, children tend to use a wider range of both human-made and natural materials to make their own dreamcatchers.

While the message of dreamcatchers is an eternal one, their appeal to Native and non-Native people alike can be attributed to many factors and a number of current trends. The Native North American people's ongoing struggle for recognition, for the return of their ancestral lands and for political rights and self-determination has brought Native issues to the forefront of media attention and political debate. Symbols, customs and languages that were once derided as primitive in comparison to European "civilization" and religious beliefs have regained much legitimacy and respect. Public interest in the background of First Nations people and culture has stimulated more discerning and sensitive research by ethnographers, anthropologists, archaeologists and historians, and it would be more discerning still if anthropologists would learn Native languages.

Euro-Canadians' growing interest in alternative lifestyles and alternative medicines—herbalism, naturopathy, shamanism—has also led to further interest in First Nations cosmology, mystical beliefs and family life. Whereas only a few decades ago it was considered a very private matter to seek psychological therapy, today it is becoming increasingly common to explore the many options available for the healing of the soul and share these therapeutic insights, methods and techniques with friends and family. As a reaction against the impersonal and alienating forces of rapid technological change and the ultra-modern mechanization of medical care in our society, more and

The never-ending interplay between the conscious self and the imagination and the unconscious self is the essence of the human spiritual condition. It is for this reason that the Native North American dreamcatcher has caught the imagination of many people.

Although the first dreamcatchers were made by the Ojibway people, dreamcatchers have become part of many different Native cultures. Today, many materials are used, including willow hoops, leather strips, mineral beads and real and dyed feathers.

more people are looking for ways to heal the spirit while tending to the mind and body. Native North American shamanic secrets, cathartic dreaming and soul searching in the Manitou world, and deep respect for the ecosystem in which the human being interacts with plant and animal have aroused the profound interest and thirst for learning of many from outside these communities. First Nations culture and spiritualism speak to people who are seeking deeper personal fulfilment, harmonious living with the natural world and spiritual restoration.

The dreamcatcher embodies all these aspects of contemporary human striving. The dreamcatcher can aid in spiritual healing; it is a constant reminder of the beauty and fragility of the natural world; it serves as a link between the unpredictable sleeping self and a mysterious sphere that transcends the self and ego. The dreamcatcher is a reminder of our smallness in the scheme of things, but it also delivers the message that even though we are powerless in so many ways, we can summon help from the unknown, the cosmic and the supernatural. When we place the dreamcatcher over our bed, we are also making a silent prayer to survive, prosper and be initiated into a realm of wonders, wisdom and magic that lies outside our reach, somewhere in the great beyond.

May the dreamcatcher bring you sweet dreams and protect you from nightmares.

In spite of the growing commercialization of dreamcatchers, they are still considered to be gifts from the spirit world, and their creators take great pride in their intricate beauty and relish the spiritual aspect of their labors. To this day it is believed that power and knowledge come through dreams, and so the dreamcatcher remains a significant contribution to our spiritual beliefs.

IN ORDER TO MAKE A DREAM CATCHER AT HOME YOU WILL NEED:

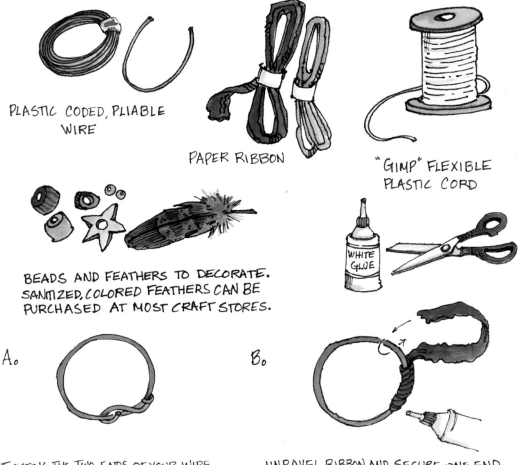

PLASTIC CODED, PLIABLE WIRE

PAPER RIBBON

"GIMP" FLEXIBLE PLASTIC CORD

BEADS AND FEATHERS TO DECORATE. SANITIZED, COLORED FEATHERS CAN BE PURCHASED AT MOST CRAFT STORES.

WHITE GLUE

A.

TWISTING THE TWO ENDS OF YOUR WIRE AROUND ONE ANOTHER, FORM A LARGE CIRCLE, APPROXIMATELY 10" IN DIAMETER.

B.

UNRAVEL RIBBON, AND SECURE ONE END TO A POINT ON THE WIRE. THEN BEGIN TIGHTLY WRAPPING THE RIBBON AROUND THE CIRCLE. WHEN THE CIRCLE IS COMPLETE, GLUE THE OTHER END OF THE RIBBON AS WELL.

WHEN YOUR CIRCLE IS COMPLETED, YOU CAN BEGIN TYING ON THE INSIDE WEB. THERE ARE VARIOUS WEB PATTERNS THAT ARE TRADITIONALLY USED FOR THIS. THE FOLLOWING IS ONLY ONE OF THE MOST BASIC FOR MAKING A DREAM CATCHER AT HOME.

C.

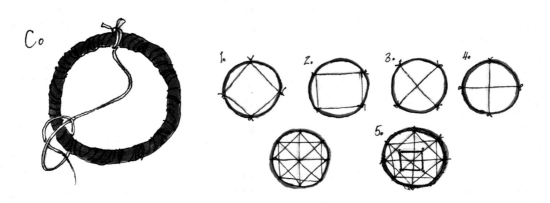

IN ORDER TO CREATE THIS BASIC WEB PATTERN, PIECES OF GIMP ARE TIED FROM ONE POINT OF THE CIRCLE TO ANOTHER. THE KNOTS FOR THIS ARE LOOPED DOUBLE KNOTS. TO BEGIN, TIE THE FIRST KNOT AT THE TOP CENTER OF THE CIRCLE. PULL TIGHTLY ON A DIAGONAL AND SECURELY TIE TO THE SIDE CORNER. FROM THE SAME POINT, TIE ANOTHER KNOT AND PULL TIGHTLY TO THE BOTTOM CENTER POINT OF THE CIRCLE. THIS PROCESS IS

REPEATED UNTIL A DIAMOND IS CREATED (1.) NEXT, OVERLAP THE FIRST SHAPE WITH A SERIES OF KNOTS THAT FORM A SQUARE. (2.) THEN AN X. (3.) AND SO ON. (5.) LASTLY, SMALLER PIECES OF GIMP CAN BE TIED WITHIN THE PATTERN TO FURTHER THE EFFECT OF YOUR WEB.

NOTE: THE BEADS MAY BE RANDOMLY, OR IN A
      PATTERN IF DESIRED, STRUNG ON THE GIMP
      DURING THE TYING PROCESS. BE SURE TO
      TIE AN EXTRA KNOT AFTER EACH BEAD TO SECURE IT.

D.

TO CREATE THE FRINGES, LOOP OVER PIECES OF RIBBON AT THE BASE OF THE CIRCLE, AND TIE THE TOPS INTO KNOTS.

E.

USING THE GIMP, FASTEN THE FEATHERS TO THE EDGES AS WELL AS THE FRINGES. FINALLY, TIE A SMALL GIMP LOOP ON THE TOP FOR HANGING.

Notes

1. Arthur Ray, *I Have Lived Here Since the World Began.* Toronto: Key Porter Books, 1996.
2. Peter S. Schmalz, *The Ojibway of Southern Ontario.* Toronto: University of Toronto Press, 1991, p. xv.
3. Peter Jones, *History of the Ojibway Indians.* London: 1964, p.37.
4. Frances Densmore, *Chippewa Customs.* St. Pauls: Minnesota Historical Society Press, 1979, p. 52.
5. Ibid.
6. Ibid.
7. Norval Morriseau, *Legends of My People: The Great Ojibway.* Toronto: McGraw Hill Ryerson, 1965.
8. Basil Johnston, *The Manitous: The Supernatural World of the Ojibway.* Toronto: Key Porter Books, 1995.
9. Ibid.
10. Ibid.
11. A. Irving Hallowell, *The Ojibway of Berens River, Manitoba: Ethnography into History.* Fort Worth: Harcourt, Brace, Jovanovich College Publishers, 1992, p. 88.
12. Theresa S. Smith, *The Island of the Anishnaabeg: Thunderers and Water Monsters in the Traditional Ojibwe Life World.* Moscow, Idaho: University of Idaho Press, 1995.
13. James McCandlish, "Housewife faces jail over gift she made for the First Lady." *National Enquirer*, August 22, 1995.
14. Florence Loyie, "Help for Dunblane's Children: Dream-catchers from Canada ease the trauma after killing." *The Toronto Star*, January 3, 1997.

Bibliography

Printed Sources
(ed.) Buswa, Ernestine et al., *Ojibwe-Odawa People: Yesterday-Today* (Manitoulin Island: Ojibwe Cultural Foundation, 1978)
Cameron, Anne, *Spider Woman* (Madeira Park, B.C.: Harbour Publishing Co., 1988)
(ed.) Cowan, William, *Papers of the Twenty-Fourth Algonquin Conference* (Ottawa: Carleton University, 1993). Oberholtzer: Net Baby Charms: Metaphors of Protection and Provision, pp. 318-331.
Densmore, Frances, *Chippewa Customs* (St. Pauls: Minnesota Historical Society Press, 1979)
Dewdney, Selwyn, *The Sacred Scrolls of the Southern Ojibway* (Toronto: University of Toronto Press, 1975)
Duncan, Lois, *The Magic of Spider Woman* (New York: Scholastic, 1996)
Geographic Board of Canada, *Handbook of Indians in Canada* (Toronto: Coles, 1974)
Hallowell, A. Irving, *The Ojibway of Berens River, Manitoba: Ethnography into History* (Fort Worth: Harcourt, Brace, Jovanovich College Publishers, 1992)
Houston, James and King, B.A., *Ojibwa Summer* (Don Mills: Longman, 1972)
Indian and Northern Affairs, *Central Cree and Ojibway Crafts: 9: Recreation and Children's Articles* (Ottawa: Ministry of Indian and Northern Affairs, 1974)
Johnston, Basil, *The Manitous: The Supernatural World of the Ojibway* (Toronto: Key Porter Books, 1995)
Loyie, Florence, "Help for Dunblane's Children: Dream-catchers from Canada ease the trauma after killing." (*The Toronto Star*, January 3, 1997)
Lyford, Carrie A., *Ojibway Crafts* (Washington: Publication of the United States Department of the Interior, 1943)
McCandlish, James, "Housewife faces jail over gift she made for the First Lady." (*National Enquirer*, August 22, 1995)
MacLean, Hope, *Indians, Inuit and Metis of Canada* (Toronto: Gage, 1982)
McMillan, Alan D., *Native Peoples and Cultures of Canada: An Anthropological Overview* (Vancouver: Douglas & McIntyre, 1995)
Morrisseau, Norval, *Legends of My People: The Great Ojibway* (Toronto: McGraw Hill Ryerson, 1965)
(ed.) Penney, David W., *Great Lakes Indian Art* (Detroit: Wayne State University Press & Detroit Institute of Arts, 1989)
Ray, Arthur J., *I Have Lived Here Since the World Began: An Illustrated History of Canada's Native People* (Toronto: Key Porter Books, 1996)
Rogers, Edward S., *The Round Lake Ojibwa, Occasional Papers 5: Art and Archaeology Division of Royal Ontario Museum* (Toronto: University of Toronto Press, 1971)
Schmalz, Peter S., *The Ojibwa of Southern Ontario* (Toronto: University of Toronto Press, 1991)
Smith, Theresa S., *The Island of the Anishnaabeg: Thunderers and Water Monsters in the Traditional Ojibwe Life World* (Moscow, Idaho: University of Idaho Press, 1995)

Multi-Media Sources
Arcane Light Productions, Native American Craft Series, *Dreamcatchers: "How-To" Design and Craft Your Own*, 1994. (video)
www.cookie.net/crafts
www.dreamcatchers.org/dcat
www.lib.uconn.edu/NativeTech/dreamcat
www.oregoncoast.com/dream/legend

Resource Centers and Libraries
Native Canadian Centre of Toronto, 16 Spadina Rd., Toronto, Ont., M5R 2S7
Native Canadian Resource Library Collection, Toronto Public Library, Spadina Rd. branch, 10 Spadina Rd., Toronto, Ont., M5R 2S7
Robarts Library, University of Toronto Library
Woodland Cultural Centre, 184 Mohawk St., P.O. Box 1506, Brantford, Ont., N3T 5V6

Index